THE CALL

AHMED HULUSI

www.ahmedhulusi.org/en/

ISBN-10: 0692756086
ISBN-13: 978-0692756089

THE
CALL

AHMED HULUSI

www.ahmedhulusi.org/en/

Translated by ALIYA ATALAY

ABOUT THE COVER

The black background of the front cover represents darkness and ignorance, while the white color of the letters represents light and knowledge.

The image is a Kufi calligraphy of the Word of Unity: ***"La ilaha illallah; Muhammad Rasulullah"*** which means,

"There is no concept such as 'god', there is only that which is denoted by the name Allah, and **Muhammad (SAW)** is the *Rasul* of this understanding."

The placement of the calligraphy, being on top and above everything else on the page, is a symbolic representation of the predominant importance this understanding holds in the author's life.

The green light, reflecting from the window of the Word of Unity, opens up from the darkness into luminosity to illustrate the light of Allah's *Rasul.* This light is embodied in the book's title through the author's pen and concretized as the color white, to depict the enlightenment the author aims to attain in this field. As the knowledge of Allah's *Rasul* disseminates, those who are able to evaluate this knowledge attain enlightenment, which is represented by the white background of the back cover.

CONTENTS

1

INTERCESSION AND DUALITY

The body has an age, but consciousness doesn't! The age of consciousness is its age of knowledge! One's age of knowledge depends on a healthy life and contemplation… So, I guess the smart thing to do is increase our age of knowledge as much as we can before we leave this world… As Rumi said, "The past has passed, my dear, today is a new day!"

They asked me yesterday about the intercession of the Rasul of Allah (saw) and why it is said to be upon the 'committers of great sin'.

Who are the committers of great sin?

I said two things need to be understood first.

People think 'intercession' is going to take place by someone grabbing hold of your arm and dragging you somewhere! Do you really think someone is going to hold you and take you somewhere?

There is intercession in this world, in the life to come, in the place of gathering and in hell…

There is the intercession of Rasulullah (saw), and that of the saints and scholars.

What is intercession? What is its purpose? Is it only to save people from hell?

What is the greatest of sins?

The verse says, **"Assuredly, duality is a great wrongdoing!"**[1]

That is, to reduce Allah to the concept of a god! This is duality!

The Rasul (saw) says "After me, my people will not openly engage

[1] Quran 31:13

in external duality, what I fear on behalf of them is the **hidden** type of duality."

Then, to worship a god is the biggest of mistakes and the root cause of all other misdoings!

Hidden duality or belief in a deity-god lies at the root of all sins.

The verse "O believers, believe in Allah" came to the companions who believed in Muhammad (saw) and the Quran, but who had not yet forgone the concept of godhood. If the companions who saw the Rasul of Allah were like this, what about us?

The way to believe in Allah and be saved from hell and hidden duality depends on our eligibility to intercession.

> **"Who can intercede in His sight except by the permission of Allah?"**[2]

If we take this as "Who can intercede except by the permission of god" our hellfire will not be extinguished very easily! We'll continue to burn and suffer!

What is the difference between the sentence, **"Who can intercede except by the permission of God"** and **"Who can intercede except by the permission of Allah?"**

Let us rephrase the latter:

"Who can intercede in His sight except by the forces that manifest from the Names in one's essence?"

To give a parable, can a treasure hidden in your house be found in another building?

How can intercession reach us when we are constantly repelling it?

So long as the curtain that's veiling our insight is pulled over us, we cannot attain intercession.

How can intercession reach us while we still believe in a deity-god and His 'Ambassador' and the Arabic book of commands sent by a god who speaks Arabic!

How can we expect intercession while wishfully thinking the saints

---

[2] Quran 2:255

of god are going to magically save us from hell with their magic wands?

If Allah (the forces that manifest from the Names in our essence) does not accept intercession, who can intercede? How will the curtain veiling our insight be removed and allow us to reach intercession? And thus, how can we be cleansed from hidden duality and truly believe in Allah, the essential reality of our being and all things, and duly READ the Quran? Is it not stated that those who are not cleansed from duality should not touch the Quran?...

My understanding is, one must first be eligible for intercession via the permission coming from one's essence. Then one must be cleansed from his external veils, and then stop doing wrong to himself, his consciousness or his essential reality.

So long as you prevent yourself from experiencing your essential reality, you are wronging yourself.

Especially if you know this truth but refrain from sharing it with your close ones, you're doing the biggest wrong to your closest and dearest!

I want to, but it doesn't seem to work!

Why not?

You can't buy cake from a plumber or shoes from a computer store!

Satan became 'Iblis' after judging Adam based on his looks! If he had been able to evaluate Adam based on his knowledge and essence, this play wasn't going to take place!

We've been created solely for the sake of knowledge!

Allah placed knowledge behind fire so the coward who fears the process of cleansing through burning does not come near it and thus only those who deserve it can attain it...

Those who surpass the fear of burning away their ego identities and dive into this fire will go through hell on the right side of the Antichrist and enter the heaven of knowledge and gnosis. But those who can't overcome their fear cannot pass through this fire and thus can't reach knowledge and gnosis. Fear must be relinquished!

So, have we rid ourselves from hidden duality? Let our conscience give the answer!

Have we understood that the One whose name is Allah is not a god;

have we at least believed it? Are we able to see and hear Him at all times and everywhere? Are we conscious of the fact we are constantly engaged in a dialogue with Him?

To attain intercession, we must first not reject what is being offered to us!

Intercession is to be freed from hell, and hell can take place not only in the hereafter but also in this world!

Intercession is to unite with Allah, which can only happen via finding a sage, one through whom the knowledge of Allah has become manifest, and by duly following his path!

Intercession is to remove the ignorance, which leads one to persistently make mistakes, and to give knowledge!

Such is intercession of the Nabi, the Rasul and the saints.

With this knowledge, a person can cleanse himself and be saved from suffering. And by living its requisites (both internally and externally), he can unite with Allah at the level of consciousness!

So, first the Allah in your essence, rather than the god beyond you, has to give permission, in order for you to become eligible and open for intercession!

Then, you can evaluate that knowledge, which itself is an intercession, and cleanse yourself by complying with it.

Then the hidden duality will end and you will unite with Allah,

This is pretty much how I answered this question yesterday. Thinking about this topic in depth, debating and understanding means the door to intercession has opened, I hope!

Forgive me if I've made any mistakes.

I leave you alone with your conscience.

"Sufficient for you is your individual consciousness at this stage to discern the consequences of your actions."[3]

31.1.98

New Jersey - USA

---

[3] Quran 17:14

2

VEILED FROM REALITY

How are we veiled from reality?

What does it mean to have concrete thoughts?

Both 'concrete' and 'abstract' concepts are based on the dimension to which they are subject.

The things you perceive via your brain are concrete things, whether they are dreams or your imagination. The measure here isn't the five senses, but rather that the brain is able to convert it into something that is recognizable and perceivable. The main criterion is that you become aware of it! As soon as you are aware of something it becomes your concrete reality, even if it's still abstract for someone else.

On the other hand, that which you can't really become aware of, or give form or shape to in your consciousness, is your abstract.

Sometimes you know of something, you can feel it; in fact, it is almost as though you can touch it, but you still can't name it or define it. That is your abstract!

Most of the terms and names we use, our evaluations and interpretations are all *relative* and point to the concrete concepts we have pre-formed in our heads based on old ideas.

The brain processes information based on its pre-existing database before we know it!

First, data comes to the brain. Then the brain takes this data or wavelength and checks it against its predetermined database. If the incoming new data is similar to that which already exists, it immediately synthesizes the two and makes an assumption based on it. Thus, new information is evaluated based on old information. And, as a result, the general output is something along the lines of, "Oh, I already know this"...

Because the same process applies to data that is uploaded to the spirit, it is said the people in heaven will claim, "These are like the things we tasted in the world"... But in reality, they are totally different things.

So, if we evaluate new things we encounter according to our old records we will be curtained from the originality of the new, claiming "There is nothing new"!

But the truth is, "There is nothing *old*!"

For, He is forever manifesting Himself anew at every instance! He doesn't revise and recreate the old!

If that were the case, reincarnation would have been true, for example, Abdulqadir al-Jilani would have come back in another form and label. Or someone else!

Rumi says, "The things of yesterday are left in yesterday," but we don't seem to think about the depth and comprehensiveness of this phrase.

We always take life as the continuation of the old, the things that were spoken of centuries ago, the values and conditions of yesterday... We don't seem to think about what new or renewed creation means, and what the scope of this entails.

Because we evaluate the new in light of the old, we automatically live in the illusory world of the past while wishfully hoping to see the concept of the past in the guise of today.

And this applies not only to our religious and spiritual lives, but also to our worldly life.

The past is important for us to take lessons from and thus know the value of the new, not so we regress and relive the past. This goes against the mechanics of the system and order of Allah.

It's one thing to evaluate the past; it's another to *live* in the past.

Are you aware that you're constricting and conditioning yourself with judgments you've made in the past and missing out on innumerous blessings thereby?

People of perfection will only output perfection!

If you see an inadequacy, judging by past conditionings, either that person is not a person of perfection or you lack the ability to see their perfection due to your own inadequacy.

Without knowing its wisdom, you compare the new to the old and misjudge. But remember, the one who compared fire to earth had failed in his judgment!

We came not to analyze and evaluate others, but to know and develop ourselves so we may move onto the life after without regrets.

Everything else besides this will slow us down from reaching our purpose and make us lose things for which we cannot compensate.

So, let us try to reevaluate everything anew, objectively, without making comparisons to the past. Let us try to see and evaluate things as though for the very first time.

This applies not only to evaluations you make in your life, but also to your thoughts, dreams and imaginings... They too are judged and analyzed based on past data, which is why we are constantly in a mode of comparison.

Does life result by renewing and revising the old or are new things actually being created, but we are failing to recognize this because our brains are always making comparisons?

But why can't we recognize the new in spite of the old?

The simplest reason is because we fail to recognize the mistakes in our current database. In other words, we're not hitting the 'refresh' button! We're filtering the new data with our old database!

If we really want to perceive the new, we not only need to refresh, but we need to format our database! This is near impossible for a brain that is working below full capacity!

So, if it's not really possible, why am I writing all of this?

Because this is what I think the situation is and I personally try to evaluate existence based on this truth and I think you should know it too. For, if we don't recognize the new, we'll have to wear the hand-me-down's from our parents and their parents and so on...

So, come my friends, let's stop comparing things to the past or to others and let's try to evaluate the new for what it is. Some associate the word sharia with comparison and Islamic consensus alongside the Quran and hadith. My understanding is sharia only comprises the Quran and the teachings of the Rasul (saw).

28.11.98

New Jersey – USA

3

INQUISITION

The ability to question is a quality that's specific to brains that can think and contemplate. It is a quality of intelligence. However, only one who is smart in their judgment can duly evaluate the results of their inquisition.

Knowledge that is the answer to an unasked question cannot be acquired! Knowledge is the due right of one who questions!

One who refrains from questioning will forever be deprived of the knowledge contained in the answer.

So, the first quality of a thinker is the ability to question and research!

Especially those things that are going to be of benefit in their eternal life to come. Knowledge that is only applicable to this world will be of no use in the life after death and we'll only be wasting our time here on earth.

A religious understanding based on blind imitation rather than authentication based on research has always been more popular. People generally prefer the easy way out, one where they don't have to think too much, and thus prefer to follow alleged 'scholars' who don't encourage them to contemplate. Unfortunately, those who duly live the merit of their humanity are very few in number.

In any case, those who contemplate and research, yet fail to find the truth, are still more valuable than those who imitate the truth. For, one who researches gains the ability to inquire into and discover new things, and uploads these qualities to his spirit, while the latter will live in a paradise that is extremely limited. Going to paradise, as I said before, does not depend on one's deeds, but what has been predetermined for him by creation.

Are we duly experiencing and fulfilling the requisites of knowledge and gnosis or are we squandering away our lives with hearsay and gossip instead?

If the knowledge we acquire isn't enhancing our daily lives, then we are only deluding ourselves; wasting away our lives engaging in more 'sophisticated' gossip to render ourselves 'different'!

If you want to experience the merits of your humanity through inquisition and contemplation, then you must first decide on this…

Are you going to fulfill certain religious requisites in order to acquiesce and please the god up there so He may reward you or to grow and develop yourself just as you eat healthy food to gain the benefits therein.

To think yourself safe on a day where "no one is going to be of benefit to any one" just because you're close to one eminent person or another without fulfilling certain requisites can only be self-delusion.

One wonders which reality of the system the Rasul (saw) was referring to with his words, "If you knew what I knew you could not sleep so comfortably in your beds, but would flee to the mountains yelling out 'Allah Allah!'"

Why did the Rasul (saw) advise against lying, gossiping, gambling, drinking alcohol and committing adultery and recommend salat, fasting and pilgrimage instead?

Ask the people around you, what is the meaning of salat? Ninety five percent are likely to say it is worshipping god, a physical activity, to appear before god, to acknowledge the greatness of god by prostrating before him, and so on…

Salat is the act of 'introspective' turning! It is to feel and experience one's essential reality! It is to acknowledge one's nothingness in the sight of the One. It is to experience your individual expression while standing, your inevitability of fulfilling your servitude before His Power while bowing, and the 'One'ness far beyond any concept of multiplicity and complete inexistence of the 'self' while in prostration.

This is the salat that opens the believer's path to ascension!

The one where a god is worshipped is nothing other than a ritual.

One can only reach paradise with faith and the application of its requisites, and Allah, to the extent he can cleanse his thoughts – of course, as much as it has been allowed for him… No one, including the Rasul of Allah (saw), has ever reached Allah without contemplation and questioning.

Salat is invalid without the Fatiha, because Fatiha is the key to this introspective turning. Turning to Allah begins with contemplation upon the meaning of the Fatiha. Whether you recite it in Arabic or another language, if you read it without knowing its meaning, it is no different to a parrot repeating it! Just like one who says 'honey, honey' over and over again, but has never actually tasted it and is deprived of its benefits. The point is to taste it, experience it, live it! Not repeat it!

Moving on…

We talked about reading the spirit of the Quran, but people thought I was referring to something else, like having a body and then also having a separate spirit.

We talked about 'reading' the Rasul of Allah (saw) and how evaluation in light of this type of reading can lead to accurate results, but people thought I was referring to uniting with the spirit of the Rasul (saw) and reading hadith!

Do we not need to inquire into the reasons of the teachings brought by the Quran and the Rasul of Allah (saw) to attain the secrets and wisdom they contain?

Why did such teachings come? For what purpose? What are we being asked to realize?

In short…

If you are capable of believing, believe. Then, immediately begin to question and research so you may reach the wisdoms therein.

Think about the reason and purpose behind your actions lest you become an imitator!

He who has been so destined will stop imitating and start authenticating!

He who isn't, will only squander away his life with rumors!

5.12.98

New Jersey – USA

4

NO ROOM FOR EXCUSE

Did the Rasul of Allah (saw) come from space?

Did he live in space?

Or did he go to space?

Did he not come from the same place we came from?

Did he not live in the same world as we do?

Did he not go to the place where some of us have also gone, while the rest of us are waiting to go?

> **"There has certainly come to you a Rasul from within yourselves, he is Mighty; your suffering grieves him... He is truly concerned for you! He is Ra'uf** (compassionate) **to the believers** (who believe in their essential reality) **and the Rahim** (enables them to live the perfection in their essence)**."**[4]

The place beyond… A God beyond… God's delivery-man, beyond… Beyond, beyond beyond!

If everything is beyond you, how can you see that which is inside you?

Like believing you're paralyzed and asking to be carried while you are perfectly healthy and able to walk! The paralysis is in your head, my friend!

Why wait for a Rasul who is Rauf and Rahim outside and beyond, instead of looking within?

---

[4] Quran 9:128

Why not dive into the ocean and try to swim as he did instead of sitting around on the sand watching and gossiping about the other swimmers?

When are you going to realize you are part of a system that has to be read, deciphered and applied?

For how long are you going to believe in a god who sends commands from the other side of the universe to his deliverer-prophets and who sends his obedient servants to paradise and casts the rebels to hell?

Does the Quran not repeatedly highlight the consequences of following the corrupt religious understanding of one's forefathers?

Translations of the Quran are always according to the understanding of the translators; they are not the original Quran! When even my own writings contain more than one meaning and thus their translation into another language can never be exactly the same as their original Turkish, how can we be so naïve as to think the revelation of Allah through His Rasul (saw) can be confined to a single meaning?

Unfortunately, those who have failed to discern the real meaning of the Quran have translated it without any depth, using words that conceal its essential meaning, whether consciously or not...

The word prayer for example can never replace the original word salat. While prayer implies the act of praying to someone, salat denotes introspective turning to one's own essence. While the former leads to duality through worshipping an 'other', the original leads to discovering the One whose name is Allah 'within' through spiritual 'ascension'.

The Rasul of Allah (saw) asked us to establish 'salat'; the Quran does not ask us to worship, it asks us to experience salat.

The purpose isn't to bow and prostrate before a god to honor and exalt His highness! It is to turn to the reality of Allah within and experience one's nothingness in the presence of that One. This is the true meaning of servitude!

It is not possible to understand 'illa Allah' (only Allah) before discerning the meaning of 'La ilaha' (there is no god). One devoid of this understanding can never truly believe in Allah, His Rasul and His revelation, the Quran.

Please realize that the root cause of all misunderstandings is the failure to differentiate between the concept of god-godhood and the magnificent system and order created by the very Names and qualities of Allah!

This is because we fail to rid ourselves of the belief in a deity-god, which has become embedded in our genes, and thus not realize that 'Allah' is not a god!

And because we think of Allah as a god, we conceive the Rasuls as 'delivery-men-prophets' who receive messages from a god up there! We fail to see the difference between Allah's prophets and Allah's Rasuls!

Also, stemming from this lack of understanding, we fail to see which mechanisms will be activated when we apply the recommendations in the Quran and what we'll be deprived of when we don't apply them!

Perhaps it's easier to assume there is a god up there, that way we always have someone to blame!

When are we going to abandon the translations based on a godhead and truly READ the original message?

15.11.98

New Jersey – USA

5

FAITH VS KNOWLEDGE OF FAITH

For most of us, religion plays a big part in our lives. We easily get protective and defensive when someone speaks adversely about our faith. But does claiming to be a Muslim make one a true Muslim? Can one be a believer just by claiming to be one? What does the word believer mean? Why do we use this word?

Faith is part of our natural composition. It's not something that is acquired later. Though it may become apparent during the later stages of one's life, this can only occur if it is already inherent in one's nature.

What does it mean for faith to become apparent in one's life?

Faith is to become aware of the ONE, beyond the illusion of the person-identity and to have the insight that all things are formed by Him.

Faith frees one from the state of hell and enables one to experience the state of paradise. Islam hastens this process, freeing the person from suffering more swiftly and leading the person to an elevated state of life in paradise.

To have faith in what the Nabi and Rasul have brought is to know that the One has disclosed information about His system through Risalah. Even a man in the middle of Africa who hasn't heard of the Rasul can attain the state of paradise once faith becomes apparent in him. On the other hand, many Muslims spend their days in prostration, yet their natural disposition is devoid of faith. Their faith is founded on imitation, which means they make the transition to the next life as unbelievers.

The first point about death is the person passes through hell yet does not burn. Burning or 'suffering' is derived from a state of faithlessness.

It can be categorized as any state that makes you upset, distressed, fearful or hateful, and makes you want to escape.

The light of faith is what enables one to realize that everything is determined, willed and created by the One, and everything is exactly the way it is supposed to be – it could not have been any other way!

This is the type of faith that will lead one to paradise, even if he has never seen or heard the Rasul (saw).

It is the internalization and reflection of faith on one's character that is of importance, rather than their verbal claim of "I am a believer."

To say "I am a Muslim" means nothing if one's state and disposition isn't saying the same thing.

As I explained in my previous writings, the word Allah is only a name. What is of significance is the meaning that it references.

One needs to consider what they believe in… In what do we have faith? How are we to understand the word faith?

Faith as understood broadly in respect of how it encompasses the whole of humanity can manifest itself as an inherent characteristic in man, and after a lengthy purification process can lead to the experience of paradise even in those that have no knowledge or understanding of the Rasul of Allah (saw).

Essentially, to have faith in the Rasul is a type of imitative faith. Even to have faith in the Rasul (saw) without believing in Allah as denoted by the letter B is insufficient and imitative!

For an imitative faith to transform into an authentic faith depends solely on discerning the secret of the letter B.

To have knowledge of faith is not adequate to experience paradise. It is like loading data regarding paradise to a computer – it does not mean the computer will experience paradise!

So, why is it absolutely necessary to have faith?

We mentioned above that faith entails the acceptance of a single creator who is Fatir; who creates all things as He wills. As such, it is not possible for anything to be absurd or meaningless or out of place, for the One creates and observes all things as He wills. This leads the person to a state of acceptance, which extinguishes all flames and ends all suffering. This is when the fire of hell says, “O believer, pass through me hastily, your light of faith is about to extinguish me”! The light of faith is what extinguishes all of the fire of hell. Notice that I didn’t say the *knowledge* of faith, but the *light* of faith, which is the state and experience of it.

When one evaluates things in this light, one reaches the state called the ‘pleased self’ (nafs-i radhiya), or in lack of it, one continually suffers until attaining the point of no more suffering.

Having knowledge of faith is not the same as having faith. Only when one has ‘faith’ rather than its knowledge can they become free of suffering and reach paradise, observing the One in all things at all times.

Knowledge of faith is like the metaphor given in the Quran of a donkey carrying books. One can carry the knowledge of faith yet continue to suffer in the face of events, complaining about why things are the way they are and why they couldn’t be different!

If you’re living with the knowledge of faith rather than its experience, your suffering will not end, even when you make the transition to the next life, you will continue to suffer!

You can only be sure that you have faith if you no longer suffer, if you are not reactive and feel the need to blame situations or people! Only then can you experience paradise. And if the secret of the letter B has become disclosed to you and you have been blessed with its experience, then you will become:

“The observing one”

20.6.98

New Jersey – USA

6

DO WE BELIEVE IN ALLAH?

"The Bedouins (those who lived based on their conditioning, in ignorance as tribes and clans) **said, 'We have believed'... Say, 'You did not believe!' Say 'We have submitted** (become Muslims)**'! For faith is not yet clarified and established in your consciousness! If you obey Allah and His Rasul,** (Allah) **will not detract anything from your work... Indeed, Allah is the Ghafur, the Rahim.**

"The believers are those who have believed in Allah, who has created their being with His Names, and His Rasul, and did not fall into doubt thereof and fought in the way of Allah with their wealth and their very beings (lives)**! They are the truthful ones** (who confirm the reality with their very lives)**!"**[5]

"O believers... Why do you say what you do not do!

Saying things that you do not practice yourself incurs great hatred in the sight of Allah!"[6]

"Neither your relatives nor your children will ever be of benefit to you! During Doomsday they will cause division! Allah is Basir of what you do."[7]

"Did you see those who befriended people who incurred the wrath of Allah? They are neither of you nor of them; and yet, knowing this, they swear upon a lie."[8]

---

[5] Quran 49:14-15
[6] Quran 61:2-3
[7] Quran 60:03
[8] Quran 58:14

> **"Neither their wealth nor their children will avail them against what is to come to them from Allah! They are the people of Hell. And forever they will abide therein.**
>
> **"A time will come and Allah will resurrect them all, and they will swear to Allah like they swore to you, thinking they have some basis. Take heed, they are the very liars!"**[9]

Let us contemplate the above verses…

The first verse makes it evident that to simply claim "I believe" because you have *knowledge* of faith and apply the requisites of being a Muslim does not necessarily mean you're a believer. In fact, such a person may be faithless altogether, for actions may well be done despite doubt or denial. That is, one may display actions contrary to one's true feelings and beliefs in order to acquiesce with the environment, out of courtesy or simply because of vested interests. One may choose to be two-faced and hypocritical rather than expressing true feelings!

Rumi says, "Either appear as you are or be what you appear as"…

Easier said than done – the consequences of aspiring to this principle could be overwhelming.

Only a rare few who truly believe in Allah will take such risks – those who have nothing to lose! For such people live only for Allah, expecting nothing from anyone. Such people have already lost everything others will also inevitably lose in the future.

They only come together and chat with others for the sake of Allah! While those who can't bear this choose to stay away from them, resorting to their assumed Rabbs, who will abandon them during Doomsday. This state of being abandoned by Allah, defined as the 'wrath of Allah', will be their suffering. This is why it's important to not preach what you don't practice. If you claim to be a believer, then you must live its consequence!

If you claim to be a believer, then you must put forward the necessary actions and comply with their requisites.

---

[9] Quran 58:17-18

If you're not applying the practices necessitated by your faith and not living with the viewpoint and conduct that befits a believer, then you're only deluding yourself.

This delusion is not going to be of any benefit to you in the future.

Your actions reflect your intention – whether or not it is for the sake of Allah.

All relations that aren't for the sake of Allah are bound to end and result in regret one day.

What does 'for the sake of Allah' mean though?

It is to be true to yourself; to live by your essential reality!

It is to live by the morals of Allah and to evaluate all things and beings based on the reality of Allah.

It is to strive to aid others towards Allah so the pleasure of Allah can become apparent on them.

A relation for the sake of Allah means to be with someone who shares this same purpose.

Being subject to divine wrath is nothing other than being blind to Allah as one's essential reality! To assume Allah's wrath is simply to burn in hell in the future; thus, failing to see the very wrath to which one is currently subject is a clear indication of this. Who can be in more wrath than one who is oblivious to the reality of Allah in his essence? The very failure to recognize and live by this is the greatest torment and punishment one can experience.

Thus, to recap, living for the sake of Allah is the natural necessity and result of being a believer, if we've been blessed with faith! As such, we must forego all forms of hypocrisy, stand by and advise the truth, and be patient with the results. We must refrain from preaching what we don't practice ourselves and practice what we preach! We must not acquiesce with our environment at the expense of our faith! We must not deify things that give us emotional and bodily pleasures, but rather live by the principles of our faith in Allah, as the verse reminds us:

"That which is with Allah is better than entertainment and trade... Allah is the best of providers!"[10]

12.7.98

New Jersey – USA

[10] Quran 62:11

7

WHY FAITH?

Either faith is apparent to someone, whereby they live with the outlook it provides and are hence called the 'fortunate' or 'happy' ones, and their final destination will be paradise.

Or faith is not encoded in one's creational program, and thus the person lives with the outlook provided by the lack of faith and is called 'unfortunate' or 'unhappy' – his final destination will be hell and his life will continue in suffering.

The faith that is inherent in one's creation will sooner or later enable the person to realize that Allah is the creator of all events and actions, and will thus end the person's suffering. Let's remember the verse: **"Let it be known with certainty that consciousness finds contentment in the remembrance of Allah** (dhikrullah; to remember one's essential reality or original self, i.e. Allah, as comprising the essence of all things with His Names)**!"**[11]

Faith is based on how the brain has been wired; it has to do with whether a certain section of the brain has been activated or not. In fact, I even believe there is a gene related to faith!

If a brain interprets a situation in the light of faith, the evaluation will be dramatically different to one that makes its interpretations without faith!

No one can deduce from the onset whether a person carries the gene of faith; albeit, his behavior at any given time may give us a slight indication for that instance. Nevertheless, even if a certain action can be categorized as being the result of faith or lack thereof, no one can know in which state a person will change dimensions (experience death), and thus it is not possible to judge one as a believer or a non-believer.

---

[11] Quran 13:28

Generally speaking, just as a life spent without faith does not promise a joyful future, one with faith does not always guarantee it either.

The Rasul of Allah (saw) gives us a number of examples worth noting.

A man who dies while fighting in battle for the sake of Allah is told he is not a martyr and his place is hell because he fought merely to display his might and strength.

Another man who is known to give a lot of charity is told his place is hell because he gave not for the sake of Allah, but to be reputable among the people.

And finally, a scholar is told his place is hell because he used his knowledge to gain the credit and respect of the people and to earn his livelihood.

So, when analyzed from this perspective…

A believer is one who acts only for the sake of Allah, without expecting anything in return. All excuses for the contrary are only the result of a dualistic perspective!

If we haven't been subject to wrath and our conscience is still active, let us question our motives and intentions! Let us call ourselves to account today before we're called to account tomorrow! Let us take a look in the mirror!

Let us take heed of the verse:

> **"Whether you show what is within your consciousness** (your thoughts) **or conceal it, Allah will bring you to account for it with the quality of the Name Hasib."**[12]

Let us be honest for the sake of Allah and not sweep under the rug the wrongs that seemingly comfort us today! Let us not forget: whatever we possess today, we're going to lose tomorrow. Is it worth chasing after small and temporary gains at the expense of eternal bliss?

Especially if we're keeping silent about what we know to be true and choose to turn a blind eye to others' mistakes out of our own vested interests…? Are we strong enough to face its consequences? How are

[12] Quran 2:284

we going to pay the price for allowing the gangrene to spread in our loved ones' lives simply because we chose to be silent and blind to their blunders because of our own comfort and short-term benefits?

Indeed, the natural result of having faith is to live for the sake of Allah, even if it means losing the world! It will make one go against all odds to save his beloveds from the fire of hell.

If a person is deprived of the light of faith, he will live only for daily comforts, he won't ponder on the conditions of life awaiting him in the hereafter. His only purpose will be to earn more and indulge more in worldly pleasures. He will give up everything and everyone for this cause, even his dearest ones.

We all seem to think the Antichrist is a one-eyed man that will come at the end of times, not realizing we are all prone to encountering this destructive energy in our day to day lives!

The Antichrist is the material world that distracts us from Allah and our vicegerency. To use our brain for the pleasures of the world is to choose the paradise of the Antichrist, while to prepare for the afterlife, to live for the sake of Allah and to experience the reality of vicegerency, is to choose the hell of the Antichrist.

Both belief and non-belief form an outlook on life that enables a certain way of evaluation, which leads to a certain way of acting and naturally brings about certain results.

Let us remember the hadith:

"Allah created some for paradise… Allah created some for hell… The Pen has dried… Each person will be guided to achieve what has been written for him!"

So my friends, all forms of faith, besides faith in Allah as disclosed by the Rasul of Allah (saw), are based on obligatory actions driven by expectations for the afterlife.

By applying these, the person claims to be displaying the deeds of a Muslim, but according to the Quran they have not yet believed!

Those whose beliefs are in the scope of the letter B and who naturally live the requisites of their vicegerency 'for the sake of Allah' are the true believers. They are also of different levels, the lowest of which is called the 'peaceful/contented self' (*nafs-i mutmainnah*).

Everyone is steadily advancing toward their own creational purpose, whether conscious of it or not! Some of us plant rose seeds and some of us plant thistle seeds; some of us expect roses to grow from thistle seeds despite having been averred to the contrary!

There is no room for excuses in the system of Allah; each will automatically live the consequences of their deeds and evaluations.

If the thoughts of future are making us suffer today, then we are bound to suffer in the future.

Those who can't evaluate the reality of intercession have no right to have any expectations!

19.7.98

NJ – USA

8

THE SPIRIT OF THE QURAN AND WOMEN IN ISLAM

Many people think reciting the Arabic letters of the Quran (without knowing their meaning) is akin to 'READing the Quran'. Some even think they are READing the Quran simply by reciting its translation. Though the aforementioned may be necessary as a preparation, READing the Quran is far beyond this.

READing the Quran is like reading the system. It's about grasping the spirit of its message.

But, how can one understand the spirit of the Quran?

For what purpose has the Quran been revealed?

What does the Quran aim to make people gain?

What kind of a life has the Quran been disclosed to prepare humanity for?

Which of the qualities of mankind does the Quran reveal?

Has the Quran been revealed to force and confine humans into a restricted lifestyle and shield them from progress, or has it come to show them the path to continual growth and development, to awaken them to their rights that have been ripped away from them, and to inform, both men and women, of the way to realize their inherent divinity?

Does the Quran aim to enable people to live in mutual respect and harmony, in continual growth and development, or to regress them back to the old?

If we can answer these questions we may begin to understand the spirit of the Quran and the gate to READing the Quran will be unlocked.

When people fail to do this, they ask:

"Muhammad came as a Rasul 1,400 years ago to a tribal community of approximately 5,000 people, most of whom were extremely primitive in thought. They buried their daughters alive, out of fear they would shame and dishonor them, and bought and sold their women, regarding them more as commodities than as human beings! Surely then, it was the issues that arose in *that community and that time* and their respective solutions which have shaped the Quran. Had Muhammad inhabited another area, say the North Pole rather than the Arabian Peninsula, the book he disclosed would have been in relation to the eskimos and their environmental conditions, traditions, issues, culture, etc.

So, how can modern man be governed by the laws contained in this ancient book, which has obviously been disclosed according to the intellectual level of that time and age? Let alone addressing future generations, these outdated laws would have rendered the book obsolete a long time ago. How can the innumerous nations of the modern world be addressed by a book that was written according to the understanding of 1,400 years ago? Is the Quran trying to lead the people to paradise by taking them back 1,400 years?"

Thus, is the 'intellectual objection' of the atheists of late.

My answer is:

As long as humanity exists, the knowledge contained in the Quran will continue to shed light to humanity and enable them bliss in their eternal life *if and only if the spirit of the Quran is understood*!

To clarify this with an example:

The core reason that underlies the drafting of a new law is in fact the 'spirit' of that law. Appropriate wording will be drafted to correctly reflect that 'spirit' and thus the law will be passed. When a judge sets out to enforce that law, they evaluate cases based on the motive driving the case and its connection to that particular law.

When a judge evaluates a case based on the letter of the law rather than its 'spirit', they will often be misled – as understanding the motive of the law is essential to its application.

Laws should be applied based on their spirit, their motive, rather than their literal sense, lest deviations occur. The conscience of the judge exists for the purpose of acting based on the spirit of the law.

The same principle applies for the Quran. One must consider the motive behind the revelation of a particular verse, who it addresses and to which event it is a reference.

It is due to our misunderstanding that we have lost the message of the Quran and turned it into the 'sacred book of centuries'. Yet, in terms of its spirit and purpose, the Quran comprises qualities that can shed light on humanity for as long as it exists; it is a timeless book!

For the most part, the Quran reveals significant beneficial information about the states of life referred to as paradise and hell, and their conditions and necessities. Secondly, it explains the reality of man and the One referenced as 'Allah'!

In my previous writings, I talked about the two sources of the knowledge contained in the Quran, namely *Nubuwwah* and *Risalah*, and that the knowledge sourced from Risalah preserves its validity throughout all times and continues to provide new insight to humanity. The chapters *al-Ikhlas* and *Fatiha* are examples of Risalah-based knowledge.

Topics sourced from Nubuwwah, on the other hand, pertain more to environmental and behavioral issues and are associated with worldly affairs, such as marriage, inheritance, testimony and retribution – laws that are only valid during one's life on earth and invalid once the person passes on.

So, let us now try to understand the 'spirit' of the Quran...

Has the Quran been disclosed to us to make us return to an outdated primitive state of life, or to encourage and prepare us for what is to come by showing us the ways of spiritual development and perfection?

Hadhrat Ali (ra), whom I believe is one of those who best understand the Quran, says:

"Raise your children not according to your current time, but according to the time in which they are to live!"

This is the vision of a person who spent his childhood and youth with Muhammad (saw) and who acquired the 'spirit' of the Quran directly from him...

As for the laws originating from the source of Nubuwwah, it is evident the primary motive, more than anything, is to establish women's rights among a people who hardly regarded them to be human, but used them more as sexual merchandise! The Nubuwwah-based laws prohibited all forms of assault and exploitation of women, and instead enabled them with the right to be 'partners' to men, gave them rights of testimony where previously they had no say in any legal matters, and empowered them with the right of inheritance.

The Quran is prevention of backwardness, termination of injustice and encouragement of continual development! For those that attempt to discern its spirit, that is...

The Quran does not present these laws as a definitive measure, but rather as the formula for further development according to changing times and conditions. For example, by limiting men's right to be wed 'limitless partners' to only four partners in marriage, the Quran established the initial stage of the process towards single-partnered marriages. By relaying the benefits of having a 'single partner,' the Quran has shown this as the target for the evolved man.

Another example is almsgiving (*zakah*). While a particular amount is advised as the minimum amount of alms payable, the verses about charity encourage the giving of one's possessions without limit.

In short, the rights given to women in the Quran are not fixed and absolute, but act rather as the foundation of a 'legal system of rights' that is open to be developed according to changing times and conditions.

If a woman, who previously had no legal say, was given the right to testify as 'one of two women' (i.e. the testimony of two women being held equivalent to the testimony of one man), this, according to my understanding, was not advised as a definitive measure, but one that can be updated as women and the community in general develop.

Giving *some* right to testimony, as opposed to *no* right, was still an enormous reform in such a primitive community. By laying this foundation, the Quran was implicitly saying, "When you begin to understand and appreciate the value of women and recognize they are also servants of Allah like yourselves, and they are also humans and vicegerents on earth, do not prevent them from having the same rights as men."

If any community or nation gives equal rights to men and women, this does not in any way go against the spirit of the Quran, according to my understanding; if anything, this is what is preferred.

That women were given half of the rights of men to inherit in those days, when previously they had no right to inherit, does not in any way mean they should not be given any more right in later times. On the contrary, a community that gives equal rights to men and women reflects the level of their development in line with the Quran.

As such, by not limiting the rights he brought to humans and leaving it open for further development, Muhammad (saw) has evidently established the fact there is no need for another book after the Quran and thus another Nabi. Thereby ascertaining he is the last of the Nabis.

To conclude, in terms of its Risalah-based verses, the Quran has brought valuable information about life after death and the path to knowing Allah. In terms of its Nubuwwah-based verses, the Quran developed and updated human rights to the maximum extent according to that time and age, yet defined this as the *threshold*, without limiting the potential for development.

This primary principle, according to my understanding, is the spirit of the Quran, as it confirms the infinite validity of the 'Book' and the indubitable fact there is no need for another book.

To confine the message of the Quran to the reforms it made addressing the communities of the time of its disclosure, thus limiting its benefits by claiming it in fact belongs to *that* time, is a grave misconception. This is the direct result of not understanding the spirit of the Quran and thus not being able to read it.

While the Quran says to give one-fortieth of one's possessions as alms, it does not forbid giving one-twentieth! This figure is only a threshold – a minimum.

Allowing women, the right to inherit half a share when previously they had none, does not in any way mean they cannot be given more. Again, this is merely the minimum. Giving equal share to men and women does not go against the spirit of the Quran; in fact, it is what the spirit of the Quran advises!

In short, the rights that are defined in the Quran constitute a starting point, with no verse or hadith claiming they cannot be increased.

When we fail to perceive the spirit of the Quran, we fail to correctly READ it, and thus get we stuck on the literal meanings of its verses and fail to recognize its actual message.

And then, with this congested perception, we claim the Quran is outdated and not in line with current times!

To construe the verses that claim freeing a slave is the biggest worship – keeping in mind enslavement was an established cultural practice in those communities – as 'Islam gives consent to enslavement' can be nothing but perversion of the truth driven by ulterior motives.

To claim Islam is a compulsive and suppressive religion when it does not accept any form of compulsion and even warns the Rasul, "You are not an enforcer upon them", is a great injustice and a clear representation of the failure to grasp the spirit of the Quran.

Democracy in its widest sense is contained only in the principles of Islam, for the Quran does not impose any form of enforcement upon anyone.

The Quran only makes *suggestions* to enable bliss and tranquility to people's lives, it tells them those who apply these suggestions will benefit while those who do not will incur a loss that cannot be compensated...

Apart from these suggestions, neither individuals nor any government has any right to enforce its application upon anyone, according to the spirit of the religion of Islam. Each person is liable to evaluate these suggestions with their own logic and intellect, to act without being under the force or suppression of anyone, and face the consequences alone.

The incorrect judgments of the ignorant and heedless due to incorrectly reading the spirit of the Quran are not binding upon anyone. On the other hand, staying away from Islam and the Quran because of these misconceptions is not an excuse.

The responsibility to read the Quran and learn the religion of Islam lies with the individual. The path to learning Islam is through the Quran, not through the actions and words of 'Muslims'. Therefore, the consequences of incorrectly interpreting Islam is binding upon the individual.

So, if the Quran has come to make men and women recognize their vicegerency potential and teach them how to fulfill its necessity, and to inform them about the conditions of the eternal life and how best to prepare for it, then most assuredly, to read and correctly evaluate the Quran is one of the most beneficial things one can do. He who does so will reap its benefits; he who doesn't, will live its consequences.

Neither the One referenced with the name Allah nor the Rasul of Allah, Muhammad (saw), needs our faith or deeds. Everything we do is for our own lives, both current and future.

Blessed are those who 'READ' the Quran and live their lives accordingly...

27.9.98

9

UNDERSTANDING THE TRUTH

Do we want to understand the Quran?

If we want to have a correct understanding and evaluation of the Quran, we must first understand the words used in it and use them in their original format.

When you're reading translations of the Quran, take notice of whether the word Allah has been used in its original form or whether the word god has been used in its stead, or if the words Rasul and Nabi have been translated as prophet… If so, know for sure these translations will not help you to understand the secrets and realities contained in the Quran! Such translations will not enable you to understand the message the Rasul of Allah (saw) tried to relay to us. It is evident the translator has not grasped the meaning of the Quran.

I have explained in various writings the word god cannot be equated to the word Allah; the two have nothing to do with each other and the word god implies an external power outside and beyond our being.

I also want to bring your attention to the word prophet. Every word that is used in the Quran has been employed specifically to denote certain meanings. The word prophet, for example, derives its root from the Persian language, used in conjunction with their conception of a deity-god. Unfortunately, it has been used in place of both the words Nabi and Rasul in most translations of the Quran.

The word 'prophet' is used to denote 'the envoy or messenger of god', i.e. the postman of a deity-god out in space somewhere.

The One denoted by the name Allah comprises the essence of all beings with His Names and attributes, perceivable and non-perceivable by us.

He who reaches Allah does so not from an external source, but from his own essential being, and understands that his own assumed being (constructed identity) is an illusion and only the One whose name is Allah exists!

Therefore, the manifest reality is the disclosure of the Names and attributes of the One referenced by the name Allah, yet at the same time, He is al-Ghani, far and free from all expressions, comprising the essence of all the Nabis, Rasuls and Walis.

Such beings articulate the reality they've attained in their own essential being, they are not the postmen of an external deity!

They have attained this level of consciousness through the activation of the name *al-Wali* in their essence.

The name 'Nabi' is not one of the names of Allah, but his name *al-Wali* is eternal.

Nubuwwah is a function that is applicable only to the worldly life.

Risalah, on the other hand, is applicable in both this world and the next.

Nubuwwah is a duty that is valid only in this world, once the Nabi makes the transition to the next dimension, his duty ends. Essentially, Nubuwwah has ended with the 'final Nabi' Muhammad (saw), no other Nabi is to come after him. But some Nabi are also Rasul, and the function of Risalah is applicable and continues until Doomsday.

Therefore, while the function of a Nabi is temporary, that of a Rasul does not end with death, it continues indefinitely, for there is no end to knowing one's self.

So, when we say the Words of Testimony ("I witness there is no God, only Allah, and that Muhammad (saw) is His servant and Rasul"), we confirm the Risalah function of Muhammad (saw), rather than his Nabi function.

Nubuwwah and Risalah are higher levels of Wilayah, similar to the ranks of a general in the army.

Nubuwwah is concerned with establishing a standard of living in the society to which they are assigned. These standards define the threshold, that is, the lowest and most basic rules and regulations. Above this is infinite. It's important to understand this well.

Risalah, on the other hand, invites people to realize their essential reality and live accordingly.

"Ulul'azm" is the name given to the exalted ones that carry out both functions.

Sainthood is to know and experience one's essential reality.

When the word Nabi is used in the Quran, it points to activities that are in the scope of worldly matters, but when a higher reality is denoted, such as experiencing a certain reality, the word Rasul is used instead.

Whatever has been mentioned in regard to reaching Allah and living its requisites, it is always related to Risalah and the Rasul.

For all that is mentioned in regard to the individual realizing and experiencing his essence, the word Wali (saint) is used.

That is, highly elevated beings who've been assigned external duties based on sainthood have been denoted as Nabi or Rasul, signifying a difference to saints who experience a state of closeness with their essential reality.

If we reevaluate things in this light, we encounter much deeper levels of meanings embedded in the verses of the Quran…

To put it another way, the saints who bring and establish new sharia laws are called Nabi, while the saints who call people to realize and experience their essential reality are called Rasul.

Sainthood isn't passed on from father to son; it is the direct result of experiencing one's essence.

When the reality on which sainthood is based becomes apparent on a Nabi or a Rasul, it is called 'revelation'; when sainthood becomes apparent on a Wali, it is called 'inspiration'.

Not only does the use of the word 'prophet' veil all such facts, but many secrets to which they point are also left concealed.

One cannot duly pray with the translation of the Quran! The Quran can never be translated into another language.

The Quran is there to be understood and experienced, any interpretation of it depends on the insight and understanding of the interpreter, whatever it may be…

This is my understanding based on my insight. Only Allah knows the absolute truth.

13.9.1998

Izmir

10

READING THE RASUL OF ALLAH

Surely the importance of READing the Quran can't be stated enough … But how about READing the Rasul of Allah (saw) who disclosed the Quran? How much of the Quran can we actually read without READing the Rasul of Allah (saw)?

In general, people, or Muslims, are not concerned with READing the Rasul of Allah (saw). They see him as one of the chosen postmen delivering information and commands from Sirius, the star on which God resides, via the courier Gabriel (!). Commands to which they unquestionably comply in order to save themselves from the suffering of hell in the future and secure their parcel in paradise!

Imagine that… An imaginary god reigning down orders, a courier-like messenger passing those orders onto the people, and the people being forced into complying, lest they get beaten, punished and executed by those who are trying to be more royalist than the assumed king… People being judged, killed or even forced into marriage in the name of this king-god…

There is no such prophet of god on earth in whom the great majorities delusively believe!

On the one hand, alternating between fear and hope, they try to obey these commands, yet on the other, they persistently try to find loopholes and ways to allow the pursuit of worldly pleasures. Such people do not question, research or contemplate. It never crosses their mind to ask why and how things are the way they are! They simply accept and believe they'll go to heaven if they obey or to hell if they don't!

What kind of hell? What kind of paradise? Obviously, they don't think about such things… The "prophet" said so, that's all that matters!

If I bow and prostrate five times a day (reciting words of whose meaning I have no idea), stay hungry for a month and obey the prophet, then obviously the creator will admit me to His paradise in return!

Plus, I spend so much money to build and adorn schools and mosques in His name, surely He'll give me a pretty palace to live in paradise!

Who cares if people don't know what the reality of religion is, if they can't find answers to their questions, if religious concepts seem outdated and invalid in modern times, and if it has become impossible to acquire knowledge without money! What's it to me if thousands are dying from hunger? What's it to me about the millions in hardship? I'm building schools for 50-100 children and spending so much money! Surely He'll put me into His paradise and give me seventy mates, seventy servants and seventy palaces! And so on… Such is religious understanding based on illusion and delusion…

The apostles of Muhammad (saw) called out to him as either "O Nabi of Allah" or "O Rasul of Allah", nobody called him "O Prophet"! The word prophet isn't used in the Quran.

Without understanding the difference between the meanings of Nabi and Rasul… Without discerning the reality of the One denoted by the name Allah… Without knowing what the Wali quality of Allah references… Without knowing the word 'sky' or 'heavens' in the Quran is a reference to the various dimensions of existence, or that the word 'revelation' does not mean something that descends to earth from space, but is a reality that is disclosed from one's essence to one's consciousness, and 'disclosure' is an ascension from one's consciousness to one's essential reality… Without experiencing all of this, how can we call the Rasul of Allah a 'prophet,' reducing him to the position of a postman?

I beg you to come to your senses!

I plead that you start thinking!

How is it possible to reduce Allah, the One who created the universe full of billions of galaxies from a single point from among infinite points, to a god who sits on a star in space with deliverymen/prophets on earth?

I urge you to re-READ the Book and the Rasul of Allah again, putting aside all of your pre-conditionings and judgments!

I urge you to recognize the consciousness disclosed as the "vicegerent" in Mecca, his system of thought and universal message!

Try to understand the conditions he was subject to and how he could have evaluated the reality and his own essence, a man with the genes of the non-deity belief system who destroyed the concept of deifying external celestial forces, a man who was designed to manifest vicegerency on earth!

An unmatched disclosure of consciousness!

A magnificent essence!

A marvelous revolutionist!

He came as the RASUL to aid people to recognize the One referenced as Allah in their essence and to live accordingly.

He came as the NABI recommending and displaying the lifestyle to free one from eternal suffering and enable the experience of infinite bliss.

Consider again…

Do you believe in the 'prophet' of God whose name is Muhammad, or do you believe in Muhammad (saw) the Rasul and Nabi of the One whose name is Allah? For know with certainty, if you want the eternal bliss of the world and the hereafter and reach the One whose name is Allah, you have no chance other than to follow the Rasul of Allah!

May Allah allow us to duly discern this truth!

29.10.98

NJ – USA

11

UNIVERSAL

The universality of the religion of Islam cannot be recognized without proper and correct consideration and contemplation…

Islam did not come to address a specific tribe and give recommendations suited to their specific lifestyle. Nor did it come to the Arabs, Turks, Persians, Malaysians or any specific race!

Islam is the name given to the universal system and order created by Allah. To the extent that people understand this system and mechanism they can attain the opportunity for a blissful life in the world and hereafter.

Those who approach the religion of Islam with their national, cultural or other local value judgments can never discern the universality of the origin of Islam.

Unfortunately, the reality of Islam has become veiled in the chaos of concepts of our modern day, and the curtain of imitations and judgments.

Out of habit we claim "Islam is universal," yet with almost all of our thoughts and actions we deny it.

What does 'universal' mean in the first place? What is a universal religion?

A universal religion is one that addresses all nations, races and cultures equally! It is a belief system free from the restrictions of any localized culture or tradition, a religion that is based on the universal truths of the universal system.

Because Muhammad, the Rasul of Allah (saw), was disclosed in Arabia, from the lineage of Abraham, his message was mistakenly mixed with and attributed to the culture and tradition of the Arab community. Under the name of 'Islam, the universal religion' people have been invited to the culture and tradition of the Arabs for many centuries! Thus, many labeled the religion of Islam as the religion of the Arabs.

On the contrary, the religion of Islam is the explanation of the universal system and mechanism by the Rasul of Allah. It is the good news of eternal bliss for those who live their lives in accordance with this system, regardless of their race and background!

Muhammad is a universal man! He invites people to the universal truths! The universality of Islam cannot be deformed or degenerated with relative and local values.

All people are inevitably subject to the universal system and mechanism of Islam, and if they don't comply with its requisites then the resulting consequences will be unavoidable.

The traditions and cultures marketed under 'Muslimism' have nothing to do with the universal religion of Islam and thus not accepted as a universal message.

It is near impossible for one who hasn't reached a universal understanding to duly evaluate the universal Rasul of Allah and his message.

On the other hand, those who attain a universal understanding will never be limited by local traditions and cultural restrictions, though they will preserve their respect for them – like Jalaladdin Rumi, Shams Tabrizi, Yunus Emre and Haji Bektash Wali…

In order to READ the universal Book brought by the universal Rasul, one must first acquire a universal viewpoint and comprehension. It's no use simply exclaiming, "Alhamdulillah, I'm a Muslim" just as claiming "I know how to swim" isn't sufficient to save one who doesn't know how to swim from drowning.

It doesn't matter how universal one may speak, or the universal words one may utter, if the words don't go past local and traditional conditionings they will have no effect in his life.

It is imperative that we urgently cleanse ourselves from our conditionings and reevaluate Islam and the Rasul of Allah (saw), not in an Arabian but in a universal light.

1.11.98, NJ – USA

12

SPACE

There's no air in space!

No water!

No gravity either!

Space is dark! Space is cold! Space is dull and insensitive!

But space is alive!

It's conscious!

It's has waves!

It encompasses hell; heaven is but a speck in it!

It embraces heaven; it nourishes and observes it!

Space is vast, it brings into existence man, jinn and angels… It observes itself in them… In air, fire, earth and water… And all forms that it brings into existence with its being…

We live with air, water, earth… We live with fire… Our fifth element is space!

We came from space, we'll go back to space… If we can make it!

Space is the divine Names! Space is the manifestation of divine attributes! Space is imagination!

It's silence, it's serenity, it's tolerance…!

You can't live without a cocoon in space! You can't disappear in space without a cocoon!

You can't face the truth of space! Because you are an earthling!

You were created with earth, nourished with earth and water, you live with fire!

You eat, you renew yourself and continue your life in a closed circle!

You, the fifth element!

Do you know yourself? Do you know your true being beyond water, earth, air and fire? Do you know your roots of space?

Are you aware of the indivisible unity of space!

You think space is emptiness, dark and inanimate… An unconscious field of nothingness…

But the breath of space is the Rahman, its sovereignty is the Subhan!

All dimensions and worlds exist and subsist with space!

Your heaven, your cocoon, your food and water, your hatred and love exist with space!

If you can free your fifth element from the conditions of the other four elements you will realize space is everything! Everything becomes manifest with the waves of space… 'I' am space!

Space manifests itself as 'I', and observes and experiences itself with itself!

But who are we, the cocooned, to know this reality?

You, O the fifth element!

You, O the fifth dimension born of matter!

The love for one's home lies in faith; come back to your home, my friend!

13

RECOGNIZING ONE'S VICEGERENCY

The purpose of man's existence on Earth is for him to duly experience his vicegerency... To do this, he must first recognize his essence and origin; rid himself of the conditionings and value judgments imposed on him by his environment. He must adopt the morals of Allah, which isn't possible unless one understands the reality denoted by the name Allah in the first place.

Otherwise an imaginary god is created in one's head – with the conditionings and judgments of the person – and labeled 'Allah'. Then the person watches himself in this imaginary mirror, consoling himself with ideas of being perfect, and leaving this place with this delusion.

Knowledge is the tool to enable the experience of what it points to!

And the experience of vicegerency is the purpose!

Man's purpose is to overcome all these obstacles and experience his reality as the vicegerent.

If you don't proactively let go of and liberate yourself from the things you inevitable have to let go of in the future you cannot find your true Self.

The way of *Tariqah* has come to an end in this time, the concept of 'master and student' is no longer valid and effective.

It's impossible to find a master who can monitor and direct all of your actions at all times.

Cleanse yourself of your delusions!

No one can be tamed and trained with a remote control!

Knowledge can be dispersed from as far as the other end of the world, and received and evaluated by brains that can perceive it. But nobody can control your behavior and monitor your mistakes; this can only be achieved through one's knowledge.

The system and order in which we live is the product of Allah's morals.

The Quran is a book given to us so we realize the system and order of Allah.

If our understanding of the Quran does not coalesce with the system and order in which we live then we have not yet READ the Quran.

When the Quran is READ, the system is realized, which then enables one to recognize the morals of Allah.

The extent to which you can become whole with the morals of Allah and evaluate others by them is the extent to which you can experience your vicegerency.

No magic stick from the heavens is going to turn you into a vicegerent or saint, these are names given to states of life, to viewpoints... If you don't have these viewpoints and lifestyles, even if these labels are given to you in gold carving, it will not change the reality of who you really are.

So, do not delude yourself with unrealistic expectations. The only thing that can come to you is knowledge and intercession. You can develop yourself by applying the requisites of this knowledge in your life.

The intelligent person is one who tries to develop himself instead of wasting his time with others. Just as sharing your knowledge is compulsory, so is not forcing others into anything afterwards.

This being the case, our duty is to evaluate knowledge realistically, without going into unrealistic expectations, without deifying people, taking heed of the warnings that are given, by taking responsibility for our actions, and accepting the truth that we can only reap the results of what we sow.

May Allah ease the path of knowledge to us.

14.6.98, NJ – USA

14

LIMITED COMPREHENSION

One day Jesus was rushing away from someone. They asked him, "O Jesus, who are you fleeing from?" He yelled out as he continued, "A fool is chasing me!"

Do not criticize a fool; he'll only attack! Whatever you tell him, he'll project it back onto you instead of trying to see his faults and mistakes…

The Rasul of Allah (saw) has never been more troubled as he was by fools!

A fool is one who fails to understand what is explained to him and who merely repeats what he has memorized.

Hell for a scholar or gnostic is to be stuck among fools.

The biggest mistake in religion begins with the concept of religious titles and figures. There is no category such as 'men of religion' only 'those who can duly evaluate religion', whose lives and afterlives are eased to the extent of their evaluation.

On the other hand, those who can't duly evaluate religion, i.e. the system in which they are living, are subject to suffering or burning (i.e. hell)…

Hell on earth is relatively easier than that of the afterlife, for one experience overshadows another experience making it lighter and easier to handle. In the afterlife, however, this is not possible, the suffering continues indefinitely and does not ease!

Another largely misunderstood concept is that of 'saints'. Most people think those who have devoted themselves to religion, abandoning the pleasures of the world, are highly elevated saints!

Pure absurdity!

Such are the saints of their imagined gods!

In truth, there is the system=religion of Allah's Rasul and those who live by it, to some extent or another, depending on their natural dispositions.

But this doesn't mean such people only engage in matters of religion and nothing else. It is foolishness to categorize such people as men of religion or saints and assume them to be outside of daily life.

All areas of life are of concern to those with highly developed cognitive skills. But the primitive person presumes others to be like himself, judging others with his limited brain capacity, unaware of the limitless potential available to others.

The research capacity the brain has in one area is the same capacity it has for all areas.

Our brain cells are capable of performing all functions outside their own function, yet we don't even understand the implications of this...

So, looking at things in this light, if we want to free ourselves from false concepts like religious ranks and titles, saints and gods, we must first READ the universal system and order, the Mother of Books and then the Holy Book, the system manual.

If one attempts to discern the Quran without understanding the system and order, he will fail to recognize the true meaning behind the symbols and metaphors employed in it.

Almost all assumed 'saints' (*wali*) are actually cases of the self-accusing self (*nafs-i lawwama*) and the inspired self (*nafs-i mulhima*).

Such people have not yet breathed the oxygen of reality, they are on their way to the One with their countenance turned towards Him, engaged in the metaphoric aspect of things. Through introspective observation, they advance towards the essence of existence.

Those who have reached the actual essence have surpassed the symbols and metaphors, they observe the reality on the whole of creation, giving their due right based on their manifest qualities.

They have cleansed themselves from all false concepts related to deities, postmen-prophets and saints. They live in the world playing whatever role required by their worldly position, and are thus in most cases, veiled from others, in terms of their reality.

They have realized, seen and are actively experiencing the reality that everything transpiring in the system deserves to be dealt with in respect of their manifest qualities, and there is no room for personal judgments and emotions in this infinite life.

It's important to understand 'personal judgments, values, concepts and emotions' correctly. Though it is a frequently used expression, it is generally not discerned well and thus not applied. I do not wish to make any further explanations, but I can comfortably say the secret and key to experiencing the reality lies in this sentence.

He for whom the comprehension of the reality has been eased will focus on this and try to understand and apply it. What's the point in forcing someone who isn't destined to understand?

However, since we do not know what has been predetermined and destined for us, we should try to live our lives as though we have been fated for certain things, putting aside the conditioning that our comprehension is limited and stop making life hell to both ourselves and the people around us.

May Allah clear our path and ease our journey!

5.7.98

NJ – USA

15

THE DIVINE SCHEME AND THE DARKENING OF HEARTS

The Quran says the hearts of men are darkened with their sins.

No 'good' or 'bad' deed is ever left unreturned!

Even an ill 'thought' has consequences!

> **"Whether you show what is within your consciousness** (your thoughts) **or conceal it, Allah will bring you to account for it with the quality of the Name *Hasib*."**[13]

Verses revealed after the above verse do not invalidate this warning; however, they state one is not responsible for what one can't control. That is, you're not responsible for a thought that may randomly pop into your head, but once you take it seriously, energize it, identify with it, and follow it through, that's when you activate the mechanism of consequences!

The interesting thing is, most people do not even realize the adverse situations they face are the direct results of their own doing! If this was truly known, then faith would become manifest by default. The system is designed so this mechanism of consequence isn't easily observable.

The great majority of people live with an imitative approach to religion, putting all their effort into the transitory things they will leave behind.

The system of subjecting one to the consequences of their deeds while still on Earth is called the 'divine scheme' (*makr*) in the Quran.

Depending on the person's intention, the consequent energy will be returned to him for as long as forty days to forty years, and in some

---

[13] Quran 2:284

cases, until the end of his life. This is called the darkening of hearts. If this action leads him to leave this abode without faith, then his heart has darkened (his discernment has been blocked), which generally refers to an inadequacy of insight to evaluate the truth.

Notice that the prohibition is in reference to an ill thought, a negative thought. That is, harboring thoughts and opinions about others that they don't deserve. Thoughts are also actions; they are the actions of the brain. And each person is responsible for their actions, i.e. their consequences are inevitable.

When a 'negative thought' first comes into one's mind, the individual is not initially responsible for it, but if they continue thinking the same thoughts, then the system necessarily begins to lock and block the brain.

The results of unduly blaming someone can range between denying the judgment and will of Allah, to losing faith altogether. And if the person dies in this state, he will make the transition to the next world as an unbeliever.

The biggest symptom of a darkened or blocked heart is an imitative approach to things, based on memorization rather than authentication, and the pursuit of material pleasures and gain – generally ranging between the bedroom, kitchen and workplace. Such people squander their lives with things that will reap them no benefit at all in the afterlife. In fact, they may even be more arrogant than before, which is the result of the divine scheme!

Sadly, however, the person is unable to fathom this, he is unable to see that he has been cursed by Allah (dispelled away); on the contrary, he thinks he has a pure heart and has thus been subject to the blessing of Allah! When he's told, he fails to understand; when grace is showered upon him, it dries away before he is able to receive it and benefit from it.

He is unable to comprehend how far he is from knowing the One whose name is Allah and how far he is from living his daily life through His viewpoint, how much suffering he is subject to because of his inability to discern the reality of fate and faith, and how all of this will lead him to hellfire in the afterlife.

If one says something offensive to the Rasul of Allah (saw), even if inadvertently, he will become blinded to the truth. If one says something offensive to any of the saints of Allah, whether consciously or unconsciously, he will be deprived of the light of sainthood altogether. Not because some exterior power will punish him, but as the automatic output of the system requisites.

A wrong thought is the direct result of a state that is contrary to the principles of faith. Continuing to dwell on thoughts that contradict the principles of faith darkens the heart even more, preventing the person from experiencing the reality. This is self-afflicted punishment!

He who does not live the requisites of his knowledge begins to veil himself with his own hands, for it's not possible to maintain one's current state. One is constantly moving from one state to another, in congruence with one's thoughts. If his thoughts are appropriate, he will move towards an advanced state and will be subject to an increased insight.

If, on the other hand, his thoughts are inappropriate, he will digress from the reality towards an imitative state of life, which is the biggest punishment one can accrue…

The divine scheme makes one who is in an imitative state think he's living an authentic state.

If one possesses the knowledge of faith, but isn't living his life in compliance with the requisites of this knowledge, he has been subject to the divine scheme, in which case, he may be saved only through repentance. His salvation is conditional upon whether he is able to give the due right of this knowledge.

Repentance is to recognize one's mistaken thought and to abandon it. Yet it is quite difficult to recognize this while immersed in it. The important thing is to not become subject to the divine scheme. For once you do, it is near impossible to become free of it, as one wrong leads to another wrong, and thus, the recognition of the truth becomes extremely difficult.

Another way to explain this is:

In the brain, various cells are engaged in various activities. These activities grow and expand in time, thus a wrong activity becomes a greater wrong by the day. It is impossible to correct this chain of wrong activities without divine support.

Therefore, it is imperative that we are in control of our thoughts and to look at and evaluate things from the perspective of Allah, or at least from the perspective of the principles of faith.

None can escape the misfortune of the divine scheme without applying the principles of faith! Only through practicing the principles of faith and repenting for one's past mistakes can one extinguish the flames of the divine scheme.

When repentance is accepted, the person is cleansed from the actions and behavior that would normally lead him to his previous mistakes. As long as this cleansing does not take place, his repentance will not be accepted. This cleansing is referred to in the Quran as 'genuine repentance'.

Genuine repentance is the only thing that can counter the divine scheme. And the sign of this is following the path of the Rasul of Allah (saw). What does this mean? Following the way of the Rasul does not mean to walk and talk like him, to eat and drink what he ate and drank, or to use what he used and abstain from what he didn't!

To follow the way of the Rasul is not to imitate the traditions of the time in which he lived. It is to continue the service he gave to humanity as the Rasul of Allah, to *serve* on his path, for his cause!

May Allah protect us from all inclinations that may lead to the divine scheme and enable us to serve in the way of His Rasul (saw)!

28.6.98

NJ – USA

16

LOVE

The lover longs to be with his beloved.

The state of the lover will become the state of the beloved... He will merge with, become one with and live with his beloved, to the extent of his love...

Because we do not really understand what love is, oftentimes we confuse **'love'** with **'like'**.

When one likes, one wants to own!

When you like something, you want to possess it and have some form of control over it. This trait is common to all creation.

Some want to carry what they like in their pocket, some want to put a leash on it and show it off, and some want to capture it and put it away... But every creature, according to its creation and nature, wants to have some degree of control over the thing they like...

Love, on the other hand, is very different...

When you love, you only want to live for your beloved!

You only want to be with the beloved, you only take pleasure from the things from which the beloved takes pleasure, and refrain from what the beloved dislikes. Your mind, thoughts, soul, entire being becomes so filled with the beloved that everything reminds you of her, even when you are by her side, you long for her! Closeness seems far! You disappear, in you only the beloved remains! You look with her looks and evaluate with her evaluation, you begin to speak with her lips! Your eyes see none but her, your ears hear none other than her voice, your hands do not reach out to anyone but her!

You want her to have her grip over you at all times, to guide and administer you, to embrace you at all times! Even bodily closeness will seem like a terrifying distance. You will long to merge with her and become a single body, a single soul, a single consciousness!

If your nature appropriates it, love will burn you until you become annihilated in your beloved... And a time will come when others will see the beloved in your face, your eyes, your demeanor, and they will say, “You have become her!”

The one who likes will want to own... But the one who loves will give up everything, even his own existence and become naught in his beloved!

And then there are some who smell love, they think they are in love! But when it comes to giving something up for the beloved, the smell of love will be washed away by the soap of attachment!

He will not be able to detach from his money, his status, his close ones... He will not be able to detach from his environment, from ‘others’!

Then he will begin to recognize faults in the one he thinks he loves... He will begin to notice shortcomings and inadequacies... First, these will change his love into a feeling of sympathy; he will begin to watch from afar sympathetically... Then, what he thought was love will eventually turn into a nice memory. This experience will show him his nature does not have the program of love and he only thought his liking was love!

If the distancing was not instigated by him but by his assumed beloved, then his sense of liking will turn into hatred. He will begin to develop the desire for revenge and sway between his conscience and feelings of vengeance, thinking he was rejected, abandoned and put through what he did not deserve.

Whereas in reality, he will only be living the consequences of the love his nature is devoid of. He likes someone for their wealth, beauty, status, knowledge and/or qualities that appeal to him, but when he cannot possess his beloved, he falls apart by the disappointment and choses to live in pursuit of his own benefits.

The lover, on the other hand, has accepted to fall apart, to become isolated and to lose his money, fame, status, friend or family... His love comes from his nature, his servitude is to love... The Creator has created him to experience love through him... Thus, he does not mind giving up his parents, his wealth, his world!

The lover loves unrequitedly!

The one who likes always expects a return! The one who likes will say, "If you live the way I want you to live, I will lavish all my wealth and possessions on you!" Such a person is devoid of love; he does not know what true love is! His only occupation is the thing upon which he has been created. He will work like an ant, mate like a monkey, care for his offspring like a lion, but he will not be able to love as much as a moth, he will not be able to throw himself into the flame of love!

Love leads to burning! Liking leads to fleeing!

According to the majority of those who like, **'love'** is a type of insanity. They will not understand it, they will not comprehend how one can go against all odds, regardless of what others say, just for the sake of the beloved. 'Insanity' they will call it...

Liking is like a hobby... Sometimes it lasts a lifetime, sometimes a few years and sometimes only a few months! But love is eternal! It has no end... Sometimes it settles and sometimes it overflows, but it never diminishes.

When you meet someone, who manifests the qualities that you contain in your essence, but which you have not yet effectuated, you fall in love. The love in your essence determines the extent of your love towards them. Most times, we are drawn to love those who reflect our own potential... And sometimes that reflection occurs from one's own essence... That is when they say, **"He has fallen in love with Allah"**...

Allah has chosen the lovers for Himself... Those who live love from their essence are the ***muqarriboon***, who have attained the state of divine closeness.

He created all things as a display of His ingenuity...

He created the beloveds to love!

He created the lovers as His eyes to observe through their eyes!

The masses will not understand this love! They will not know this is love!

The true lovers are those who, like moths, throw themselves into the flames of love, and annihilate themselves in Him, and thus become everlasting (*Baqi*).

They are those who have come with a special code; they have come to fall in love! The world and its possessions will not mean a thing for them. They will never strive for worldly achievements. The call **"Say Allah and leave the rest"** is what they live by.

It is they who live love in the real sense, and through them, He experiences love, sympathy, mercy and compassion, for these are the qualities with which he created them!

But come, my friend, let us go back to our world, these fairytale-like words have soaked us, let us dry up... Let us go back to our world, strive, labor, struggle and work strenuously to please and flatter others! And then claim we are doing all of this for the sake of 'god', pardon me, for 'Allah' (!) and comfort our conscience...

If the heart has not been created for **love**, what is the point of all this talk...

To amuse ourselves with religious hobbies?

2.8.98

New Jersey – USA

17

SIGHT

Our ability to see is one of our most significant functions. But what does sight really mean? How do we see? What do we see? What do we not see?

Does everyone see the same things?

Why do some see things others can't?

How do we see in our dreams?

How do some see jinn?

Can angels be seen? If so, how?

Can one see the countenance of ALLAH? How?

What is hallucination?

What is a nightmare and how does it form?

How are we going to see in the realm of the grave?

How will sight work at the place of gathering (*mahshar*)?

How is sight in heaven and hell?

And so on and so forth…

Let's begin with remembering what sight actually means. If the waves that reflect from the objects in front of us are between four-thousandths of a centimeter and seven-thousandths of a centimeter, our pupils convert these waves into electromagnetic signals and transmit them to our brain. Then, based on the existing database, a synthesis is formed and an image is generated. This imaginary image is what we claim to 'see'.

The brain begins to receive and store external data while still in the womb. Every new data input, i.e. all waves that we perceive or don't perceive, is stored inside the brain, in an area of similar frequencies and cell groups.

All data waves stored inside the brain are synthesized with existing waves to form new compositions at all times. A wave composing a thought, for example, may be voluntarily directed to the person's center of vision and synthesized to form images. Depending on the brain's program, this may also be involuntary, in which case we begin to see illusions or hallucinations.

There is a significant difference between hallucination and the sight of saints, Rasuls and Nabis. Drug-induced hallucinations are driven by jinn and they comprise baseless ideas not supported by the system. Such ideas and images have nothing to do with the reality of the system in which we're living.

The unveiling experienced by saints, Nabis and Rasuls, on the other hand, depends on waves comprising the primary principles and realities of the system.

Please allow me to emphasize once again:

The idea that our spirit came from the heavens, from the spirit of god, that it sees and knows with the divine powers it possesses, that it's going through a trial in the body and that it will return to god – at which point it will be judged and either sent to heaven or hell – and that we see and hear through this spirit, is nothing but a misevaluation and an erroneous interpretation of symbolic expressions.

We must come to our senses and learn to READ properly... The Rasul and Nabi have disclosed the system and order of Allah under the religion of Islam, using symbols and metaphors where necessary. The Quran is the book explaining the universal system and order of Allah.

Thus, we would be wise to look for the answers inside the very system we're part of rather than searching outside.

To reiterate, the brain thinks, feels and sees within the limitation of the data waves it receives. While doing this, it simultaneously uploads all of this information to the wave-body we call the 'spirit'.

But, if the spirit is composed of waves, how does it stay as a single unit without becoming scattered?

Just as the cells composing our body are electrically attracted to each other, the same law of attraction applies to the brain, and since the brain produces the spirit, the same quality is passed to these waves, ensuring their unified existence. Hence, the spirit body will continue its indefinite existence in the afterlife as a single unit.

Let's now analyze the act of seeing that isn't based on the eye... That is, imaginations, hallucinations, dreams, visions, revelations and insights.

Dreams result from the stimuli the brain receives from the angelic and astrological effects that take place during the night, which are synthesized with the relevant data forms in the brain, then transmitted to the brain's center of vision at specific intervals to generate the images we see in our dreams.

Dreams need to be interpreted by qualified people because they are symbols based on the person's database; they need to be decoded.

Hallucinations can be triggered by drugs or jinn. The brain circuitry responsible for illusion turns the accumulated data of one's local culture and values into symbolic images. Illusions (thinking something exists while it doesn't or vice versa) can be triggered with drugs or jinn-based waves, driving the person to see things that don't actually exist.

Unveiling can be of two kinds: either with vision or without... Unveiling is the ability to evaluate and READ the system based on one's genetic capacity and database. If these evaluations are passed to the center of vision through the filter of one's database of local values, then the images that are generated need to be interpreted...

If, on the other hand, the center of vision is not involved, then there's no need for interpretation. This type of unveiling is also known as an introspective observation, insight or epiphany. Consequently, the person gains insight into the inner mechanics of the system and order of Allah.

Revelations can be also divided into two general groups: those with vision and those without. Revelations are formed via angelic means. It is known that angels are formless beings, yet it is also known that Nabis who have received revelations have often seen angels, for example Gabriel, in the form of a man.

The reason for this according to my understanding is:

Sometimes, during the process of READing, certain realities become disclosed in the brain according to one's brainpower and database, and transmitted to their center of vision as symbolic forms. Thus, the person thinks he has received this information from that form, or he deliberately says this to not contradict the general conception of the masses.

Sometimes the person emits these waves outside so forcefully that others in the vicinity are also able to see the same form. Similar experiences occur among those who claim to see UFOs. The waves comprising the image generated in one's brain is emitted to his surroundings enabling others to see the same thing.

As such, during the process of revelation, Nabis and Rasuls have seen angels as symbolic forms generated by their database. For we know neither Gabriel, the angel of revelation, nor Azrael, the angel of death, nor any of the other angels have physical forms, they can only be perceived as forms according to the observer's database.

Having shared this information, I hope I was able to stress the fact that seeing isn't the point, but it is the proper evaluation, comprehension and application of knowledge in our brain.

20.9.98

Antalya

18

WHERE IS 'INNER' SPACE?

We talk a lot about inner and outer experiences. But where exactly is this inner space?

At which point of outer space does inner space begin?

Or, after what point of inner space does it start to become outer space?

Where is the border between 'inner' and 'outer'?

It's a big mistake to think of these spaces as locations. There is no difference between inner and outer spaces; they are not in different dimensions. Inner is merely the part we can't perceive even though we see it. That is, even though something is within the range of our visible sight, sometimes we don't perceive certain aspects of it. This unperceived side is what we refer to when we say 'inner'.

But how can this be? How can one see something yet not perceive it?

When one's database isn't sufficient to decode and evaluate the incoming data!

So, in other words, when we say inner we are actually referring to all the data we are unable to perceive through our five senses.

Data reaches the brain through four ways:

a. The five senses

b. The jinn – This includes all conscious beings within the scope of the word jinn (i.e. all invisible beings), including those on this planet and others.

c. Astrological effects

d. The essence of space or universal consciousness.

The last two can be referenced to as 'inner,' while jinn can be grouped into two types:

1. The type I talk about in my book *Spirit Man Jinn*

2. Higher conscious beings residing within the solar system or other stars within the galaxy. Only those who experience self-discovery and unveiling can communicate with this type, though many who communicate with jinn mistakenly think they've achieved contact with the latter.

Let's now talk about the essence of space: universal consciousness.

This is the space of absolute unity! Absolute consciousness! The Grand Spirit! This is where we realize that space – infinite universes within one another – is the extension of our body.

This is the 'point' from which Allah has created all things.

Its end is relative. It has no end.

In respect of its intellect, it is known as the Reality of Muhammad.

In respect of its spirit, it's called the Grand Spirit.

The Names comprise its spirit.

This is where the one who experiences 'ascension' actually ascends.

This is the purpose of salat!

This is the space of oneness and unity…

Those who reach this space and find their essential selves are referred to as the *Rafiq-i A'la* (the Highest Company).

The Raised Platform (Maqam al-Mahmud) becomes manifest with it!

The angels who have attained the state of divine closeness (*Malak al-Muqarrab*) are under its command!

The worlds in the sight of this space are nothing but a dream… A hologram…

Neither angels nor Nabis and Rasuls who have attained divine closeness can intervene once one reaches this space.

Those who have not attained divine closeness will think this is the reality denoted by the name Allah!

Yet Allah can never be limited by anything!

The One denoted by the name Allah is free from the worlds!

Though 'inner' is what man can't perceive; in reality, inner is no other than outer, what we think of as implicit is no other than what is explicit, and vice versa. As soon as we perceive an implicit reality it becomes explicit. In other words, the only thing that changes is perception.

Names and labels we give to explicit things, or our conditioning regarding them, veil us from their reality and lead us to think they are implicit.

To put it another way, what you comprehend is explicit, while what you can't comprehend is implicit.

If you can observe the reality of the things around you, then their implicit reality will become explicit for you. So long as you fail to make this observation, the explicit reality will remain implicit for you.

Come my friend, come and re-format and re-program your 'self', for the program with which you leave this abode will be the program with which you'll have to run for infinity!

There will be no further opportunity for changes.

Allah knows best!

Night of Ascension - 1998
NJ – USA

19

"AFTER"

I will be in the presence of Allah *after* I stand for salat…

We will see our Rabb *after* the realm of the grave and the place of gathering…

We will see the afterlife *after* we die...

What a troublesome word, 'after' – it keeps taking us away from the present moment!

We wander off into places beyond to find the answers for many important questions.

If we've placed the angels among the stars, thinking the word heavens in the Quran refers to space, and if we assume the name Allah references a god in space who frequently intervenes into our lives via His angels, then surely the word 'after' (in a religious context) will denote nothing other than its literal meaning for us, like drinking water *after* eating!

Whereas the religious connotation of the word 'after' means *the lower dimension after the higher dimension.* That is, the dimension of the body is the world (outer or higher dimension) and the dimension of the afterlife is the realm of consciousness (inner or lower dimension).

Thus, to see one's Rabb in one's consciousness is to see one's Rabb in the afterlife.

What is the meaning of "Only the Creator will remain after the creation is annihilated"?

How and when will the reality "Everything will become inexistent, only the face of HU is eternal" become manifest?

Does "Allah does as He wills" mean "God does as He wills"?

Where is the *Fatir*? In space? Or in our disposition?

What does the hadith "*After* the 'I' dies everything will die, all the Rasuls will pass out, even the Rasul of Allah (saw) will cling to the pole of the *Arsh* in a semi-fainted state" mean?

In short, if we can re-evaluate things in light of the dimensionality denoted by the word 'after,' how will our understanding of the world, the grave and the afterlife change? How will we conceive heaven and hell?

Where, how and *after* what will we see the reality denoted by the name Allah?

9.8.98

NJ – USA

20

HOW DIFFICULT IS IT?

How difficult is it for us to comprehend certain truths?

How difficult is it for us to discern and evaluate the truths we read, memorize, talk about and observe?

How difficult is it to turn away from the world and its governments and turn towards Allah and the life after death, to which we'll travel all alone?

Let's remember:

A government is an organization that is established by the people for the purpose of protecting human rights and providing services to them. It's not sacred; it's open to modification by the people.

A government cannot have a religion. A religion cannot have a government!

A government is an organization established by the people for the purpose of governing and providing services to them, regardless of their religion, language, race and color. Those who are actively part of this organization have no divinity, immunity or privilege over others; exploiting their position for the sake of their personal gain is treachery and a betrayal to the people and the trust.

The government has no right and jurisdiction to impose a religion upon the people. In fact, the government must stand at equal distance to all beliefs while allowing the people to freely practice their own religion without pressuring or burdening each other.

The government must respect all behavior that does not violate human rights.

The sole purpose of a government is to serve the people; it cannot be biased or enforce things upon any community. A government that does not serve the people is one that has lost its purpose of existence. A government cannot request something that goes against one's faith, whatever this may be.

Religion is the system and order of the One referenced as Allah, disclosed by the Nabis and the Rasuls, to aid people in the preparation of their eternal lives.

According to the Quran, if one believes and fulfills the requisites of his faith, he will be in a state of bliss after death. If he puts forth the contrary, he will be subject to suffering.

Furthermore, religion tells us man is a vicegerent on Earth and therefore should quit looking for a deity-god in space and discover the reality of the One whose name is Allah in his own depth.

Religion does not advise oppression and enforcement. It is an invitation, an offer made to the sound and intelligent. Whether one takes it seriously or not, its consequences bind only the person.

Religion addresses the individuals, not the government.

It is the individual alone who will resume his life after death; therefore, it is the individual who needs to prepare himself.

The government is not the addressee of religion. The government has no right to intervene in anyone's faith. It must exercise its law and jurisdiction to serve the people as a whole, without invading the rights of the individuals.

The people and the government must know that any action that is enforced upon others will eventually backfire and hit the enforcer.

The people need to be notified of the essence of religion, but whether they accept it and apply its requisites is up to their own discretion.

Everyone shall die and continue their journey after death on their own. A new state of life will commence after Doomsday and everyone will pass through the dimension of hell, after which a group of believers will escape to the dimension of heaven. This is so based on the teachings of Islam.

Whether an individual will go to heaven is not determined by their actions, but by their level of faith and attitude based on this. An inadequate application of the practices of faith does not render one faithless. One will not be called to account for things he is unable to do due to non-permissive circumstances, but he will live the consequences of what he chooses not to do.

Every application done out of pressure and force is an act of hypocrisy. The religion of Islam advises that people only practice things they sincerely and genuinely believe in, for the sake of Allah, without expecting any return from anyone. One who is forced to apply religious practices is in danger of losing their faith and dying as an unbeliever.

Faith has two levels for Muslims (those who accept Islam according to their understanding of it):

a. To be freed from the suffering awaiting one after death with minimum loss and to reach eternal bliss.
b. To attain eternal bliss by reaching the One whose name is Allah in their essence and becoming moralized with His morals.

Both results can only be reached through the work one does in this world; nothing can be done after death in this cause. No Rasul or saint can give the reward for an action that hasn't been put forth during one's lifetime. There is no recorded information regarding an increase in one's level through intervention after death.

When one dies, he will realize that his entire life on Earth was only a few moments long, and the life of the world was his only chance of attaining the things he needs after death. If he hasn't duly prepared, he will feel deep regret as he will no longer have the opportunity to change things and thus will want to go back to the worldly life. But alas, this will be impossible.

This is why, if one is a believer while pursuing his life on earth independently, he must work towards his life after death. Everyone will only be given the results of what he does; nothing more, nothing less.

Therefore, the believers should stay away from aspiring for worldly fame and sovereignty, power and expectations from others, and work towards a blissful eternal life, spreading and encouraging peace and love.

A believer's purpose in this world is to know Allah, prepare for his eternal life after death and share his knowledge with others. They should not have any time to argue and dispute with others.

There is no class or status in religion. Only people who share for the sake of Allah unrequitedly. All ranks and evaluations besides this are fabrication. Only Allah knows who the saints are; we can only assume. Our concern should only be knowledge and righteousness.

Because people fail to realize that only through their own effort can they attain success and eternal bliss, for centuries they have awaited a savior (mahdi), squandering away their eternal lives.

Instead of waiting for a savior, we must work towards increasing our knowledge and applying its requisites; this is the only intelligible way.

Let us always be mindful of the fact that only knowledge that is discerned and applied can be useful.

Let the governments do their job – serve the people.

Let the people freely practice their faith without invading the rights of others.

26.7.98

NJ – USA

21

THE UNIVERSE VS YOUR COCOON

On a planet called Earth, among hundreds of billions of stars, in a galaxy amid billions, 'your world' was created!

Do you live in the world or in your world?

How much of your life is spent in *the* world and how much of it in *your* world?

From the moment you're born until the point you die, you're inside a cocoon you call the 'world'… A world created with your five senses, conditionings, value judgments and the emotions formed by them!

Are you aware of the difference between *the* world and *your* world?

Are you ready to step out of your cocoon and see the real world?

Are you sure you want to leave the comfort of your delusive world in which you don't need to question or research anything, where you're happy with your loved ones and possessions, and an imaginary god who bestows favors upon you?

A cocoon is woven with one's genetic data and conditionings, a prison in which one's connection to the universal truths is ceased!

An abode of denial, where the Rasuls and the system of Allah are unknown and the universal truths are ignored and denied! As if the teachings have never come, as if the people have never been warned of 'the day in which every soul will abandon their loved ones with the panic of trying to save themselves'… Neither the infiniteness of the universal dimensions is known, nor the fact there is no room for 'feeling sorry' in this system! People live only for money, power and sexuality! And they try to discern the afterlife by comparing it to this dream… Our dreams are no other than the reflections of our thoughts during the day. We dream the life of our cocoon and we believe it to be to true, thinking the afterlife is similar…

How do you feel when you see others in poverty and suffering? How do you continue your life after seeing this? And how about when others see you are suffering, how do they continue living obliviously? How is it that so many people with such incredible qualifications end up in need of others who are much less qualified?

Believe me, my friend, the afterlife is nothing like you imagine it to be! Hence, the truths have not been openly revealed. Hence, symbols and metaphors have been employed! Trust me, the truth, outside your cocoon world, is beyond your imagination!

If by "All of the fires of earth are but one in a thousand compared to the fires of hell" you conceive literal flames of fire rather than the conditions and events that cause one to suffer, then you're missing the point, my friend...

I wonder if I'm encouraging you to contemplate... What type of conditions and events can cause one to suffer a thousand times more than all of the fires of earth? Think about it... What causes you to burn? Why?

If you can't escape this fire by abandoning your world, if you can't become a butterfly and fly out of your cocoon, then expect to be thrown into the fire! Just like caterpillars that are thrown into boiling waters with their cocoons!

Surely, I'm not telling you to abandon the world altogether, all I'm saying is, at least spare a few moments of your day for genuine contemplation and try to understand the realities referenced by the religious symbols and metaphors.

Don't take my words for granted, go and do your own research; think, contemplate, come out of your cocoon and fulfill the due of being human! Realize that the universe isn't orbiting around the world; you're not the only species alive in this universe!

You're journeying to a place where all of the people who have come to and gone from earth do not even form a tiny colony! And if you've not acquired the right equipment for this place, then you're in trouble, my friend. Serious trouble. I'm not telling you this to frighten you, but to encourage you to think and take precautions. I'm not telling you anything different to what others have said in the past. I'm only sharing my understanding using the language of today.

If you're burning and suffering now in this world, for this reason or the other, know that your suffering is going to be amplified on the other side. Neither your money nor any of your possessions can save you.

Come, my friend, leave your cocoon and realize the universal truths.

Cleanse yourself of the conditioning and values that cause you to burn and suffer.

These are like gas instilled within your cells ready to be scorched alight with the strike of a match. If you can't cleanse yourself from this gas in this world, you will burn again and again indefinitely…

Come to your senses and recognize your vicegerency lest you create your own hell. For this is the unchanging, immutable system and order of Allah.

7.3.99

NJ – USA

22

OUTSIDE

It's too crowded **outside**... And so noisy!

What does the word 'outside' mean to you?

I don't know about you, but outside for me is definitely very crowded and noisy!

Tardigrades, also known as **water bears**, are water-dwelling, segmented micro-animals that can survive in extreme environments, like pressure about six times greater than that found in the deepest ocean trenches and physically or geochemically extreme conditions that would be detrimental to most life on Earth. Tardigrades and other such animals come to life, dwell and die in micro-cities under our eyelashes or in our eyes, ears, armpits or various other parts of our body... Putting all this, and other bacteria and viruses and basically all forms of life perceivable by our five senses, aside, let's come to the fundamental question: Where are we in respect to all the lifeforms we can't perceive? Are we really in empty space on a planet called Earth? Or are we inside the eyes or ears of some gigantic being? Who knows how many lifeforms and beings unperceivable to us we're living among? Shame we're limited to only what we can perceive with the five senses! If only we knew the answers to the questions science and medicine hasn't yet figured out!

What is our position amid all the conscious beings ranging from the microorganisms to the macro-galactic beings? Who and what are we exactly living among? Who perceives us, as what? Who and what aren't even aware of our existence? And who are aware of those who aren't aware of us?

What part of the zygote defines the color of our eyes and hair? Where and how is the tone of my voice determined? What part of that first formed cell contains the information regarding my neurons and their role and function?

A fool cannot discern 'fate'. The ignorant will refuse it altogether.

The science of genetics today displays such an immaculate record of predestination that rejecting fate can only be the result of pure ignorance.

Obviously, those who haven't yet forgone their conception of an external deity/god must think this predestination is written with a pen, or that perhaps the angels do the writing as god dictates the fate of all the people on earth!?

May we be enlightened with the *nur* of Muhammad (saw)!

May we truly understand him and discern the reality of the metaphors and examples he presented…

May we comprehend the *Batin* as the knowledge of Allah comprising the essence of all the infinite universes and understand whether the corporeal worlds are the actualization of this potential knowledge, or whether it's the observation of a conscious observer.

Let us try to understand what "The Observer is Itself" means.

Let us think about the genetic code perceived by the five senses and what it represents in the material world. What does this physically perceivable code represent in the non-physical and unperceivable world?

Where is the dimensional depths?

Where is the pre-eternal knowledge bank?

What is the 'Pen' that writes?

What is written?

What is the relation between the spiritual realm and the genetic chain?

Where does this chain begin and where does it end, and what part of it do we occupy?

How was my fate and life determined before I came into existence?

Where did Nostradamus get his information?

What was the source of his prophecy? How did he attain it?

Where is outside, who are outside and beyond us?

Among whom are we going to be when we leave this realm? Where is outside going to be then?

Are 'others' only the jinn? Or does this word refer to a much greater scale of conscience existence than we think?

Who are the others that live inside hell, an environment of such intense heat that can evaporate millions of our Earth in an instant? What are they like?

Who are the others among whom we are currently living?

And who are all the other 'others' among the billions of galaxies beyond heaven and hell, others to whom such concepts have no relevance?

My friends…

We are on an infinite journey to planes of existence our imagination cannot fathom, to a life in which this worldly life is not going to have the least meaning… We have no idea of the infinity that lies before or the infinity that lies after our current life. But one inevitable day we are going to have to leave behind all that we feel attached to, all our possessions and loved ones, and take our place among completely different 'others' in a completely different dimension.

Please think again, in light of these truths… How ready are you for this life? How helpful are your predestined qualities? Are they in favor of this life or against it?

Blessed are those for whom preparation for the afterlife has been eased!

18.3.99

23

COOKIE-IDOLS

Hadhrat Omar narrates:

"During the days of ignorance, before we understood the essence of Islam, we used to make idols out of cookies which we would worship and when we got hungry we would eat them! Remembering this makes me laugh."

How can I explain that supposedly changing one's world without breaking out of their cocoon and seeing the real universality isn't really possible!?

Raised in an environment with cookie-deities and bedtime fairytales about god, people only worry about how better they can eat and mate while practicing their 'religious duties' out of fear and suppression – hoping to be saved by cookies!

Idols and deities are the products of cocooned people, and imitators adopt these gods and become consumed by them. From the most innocent and harmless gods, like stars and singers, to the most dangerous ones, such as dictators and autocratic institutions, all such 'holy' beings and entities who seem to be so untouchable are mere cookies, waiting for their inevitable turn to be eaten!

One who has READ the essence of Islam does not need the respect or approval of imitators and humanoids. They are too busy observing Allah and His manifestations, they have no time or interest in other things. Yet they are so few in number as to break one's cocoon, to cleanse one's self from imitation and to turn away from the false and temporary paradise (of the Antichrist), is not an easy accomplishment! Such eminent ones no longer have gods and deities, for they are the servants of Allah. The god of the people means nothing to them, they expect nobody's respect or honor, nor are they fond of such things! They don't care whether the imitators accept them or not. They travel through the world as though they have stopped by to have a moment of rest before they continue their journey. They don't like titles and ranks, nor are they affected by the 'divinity' and 'sacredness' created by imitators.

Societies create concepts of divinity and sacredness, gods, laws and rules! Then they talk about the merit in serving these concepts! But when the creators of these concepts are left to themselves, they merely mock and laugh at them. These concepts, or these cookie-gods if you will, are their tools of control, they use them to control and manipulate the people, for their own vested interests! Such 'elite' ones exploit the teachings of the Rasuls and use them to advocate their own divine and sacred values!

Money, for instance, the greatest god! One who has the most servants! Then sexuality! The second greatest! A must in every cocoon! All cocooned servants deify and worship these gods, in fact their entire lives are based on them.

It seems too difficult for them to ponder on the possibility of the universality outside their tiny little cocoon…

Indeed, I had heard it's impossible to explain:

That the sun never rises or sets, these concepts exist only due to the rotation of the Earth…

That the tears of a lion eating its prey or the tears of a crocodile are not out of pity, that there is no room for pity in the animal world…

That an apple does not fall from a tree out of its love for the ground…

That sexuality is no other than hormonal stimuli…

That to love and to like are not the same, and to want to extinguish one's self in his beloved is far from the want to own and possess what one likes…

That gods and sacred values have no meaning or validity in the real world, outside the cocoon…

That environmental conditioning is constructed by those who want to drive and control the societies for their own personal benefits…

That the real world beyond one's cocoon is the world of universal consciousness…

That wisdom cannot be attained by slavery…

That sages give value not to the imitators who stand in awe and admiration before them, but the conscious ones who realize the truth and try to become real humans…

That humanoids and imitators who live only for their personal and bodily pursuits will never be able to leave their cocoons once they change dimensions…

That no sage or saint can intervene and take you out of hell and place you elsewhere, unless one genuinely evaluates and applies the knowledge and wisdom disclosed by them…

That evaluating such knowledge is not the same as memorizing it…

That a life spent worshipping sacred cookies in a cocoon is the biggest irreplaceable loss…

That only a real human, one who is created for Allah, can truly turn away from cookie-gods and find the reality of Allah…

That those who aren't human, those who are slaves to money and sexuality in their cocoon world, will never gain anything at the end, even if they spend their entire lives with stories and fairytales of wisdom and knowledge…

That political, religious or cultural authority is no other than a societal construct-cookie.

That those who don't die before death and come back to the life of knowledge and wisdom will never reach the universality outside their cocoon…

That the way of knowledge is a way of life, and should not be confused with the knowledge of a computer.

That the disclosures of the intimates of Allah (*ahlullah*) have been distorted and exploited and turned into god-cookies to manipulate and control the masses…

And on and on…

Yes… I had heard about the difficulty of explaining all of this to humanoids and imitators, i.e. to those who aren't human.

5.2.1999 , NJ – USA

24

IMPOSSIBLE

It's quite impossible for a humanoid to duly understand and live the requisites of being 'human'.

Humanoids spend their lives either acting out of their instincts or by imitating humans. They can't understand the inner works of a human. They simply think humans are like themselves, and thus evaluate them based on this awry comparison.

A humanoid's life is based on their 'identity' and 'body'. Their sole purpose is to live better, eat better, mate more and own more. Thus, they see all things that serve this purpose as licit. The only thing that can limit a humanoid is 'fear'! Without fear, they have no limits. Their main characteristic is imitation.

They don't have the capacity to contemplate and comprehend the One denoted by the name Allah. Thus, their lives are centered on their body. Eating and mating are their biggest pastimes. A humanoid male thinks he owns his woman. And a humanoid woman is possessive over her man. The concept of making love, uniting as one and sharing a life does not exist for them. Such men carry their woman around like an ornament and use them as tools in the kitchen, in their beds and sometimes in their offices. Such women live just to survive or to simply secure themselves financially and materially.

It's all about owning, mating, multiplying and having power over one another by using their bodily qualities and/or their ranks and positions. Life is a trade for them: buying and selling houses, cars, women, etc. A humanoid man owns a woman and spends his life between the kitchen and bedroom, and a humanoid woman prides herself in having a man that chases her between the kitchen and bedroom. Such helpless and desperate women usually tell their men, "Even if you get tired of me and have affairs with other women, don't leave me, come back to me, go quench your desires with others, but come back to me at the end!"

This is the expression of a serious failure of femininity and the summit of impotence. This is the beseeching of a servant to her master. This is the announcement of a total loss of self-esteem and honor.

When humanoids like someone, they do whatever necessary to own them. But they have no quality in their brain and soul to share with their 'man' or 'woman'.

Humans, on the other hand, have partners, their 'equals' in heart and soul, their travel mates in life with whom they become one.

Humans love.

Contrary to humanoids, humans share what they own with others. For humanoids, the only thing of significance and concern is 'owning' and 'price tags.'

Humanoids, who also carry human bodies, think being a human is being like a lion when it comes to ruling, a hyena when it comes to taking, an ant when it comes to collecting, a fox when it comes to cheating, a monkey when it comes to imitating and a bear when it comes to living.

Humanoids exercise and maintain their power and ownership over others through force. Humans, on the other hand, travel together for as long as they can share with one another; once they no longer have anything to share, they simply go their own ways.

Humanoids have a tribal mentality, they force, bully, impose and manipulate. They are despotic and compulsive despite how modern and human they may appear!

Humans, on the other hand, are civilized. They don't use force and they are not compulsive. They make offers and respect others' choices.

Since imitation is the main element for a humanoid life, even when they become involved in religion and spiritual topics, they do so out of imitation. Though they may be intelligent, their lack of intellectual capacity renders them unable to make intellectual decisions to find the truth. So, they simply look at how such and such eminent person lived in the past and copy them.

People of imitation can't understand and evaluate the people of authenticity. Thinking others should be like themselves, they conceive anyone who acts contrary to their way as deviant.

Fear of god for imitators is all about hellfire and suffering, while paradise is a mating environment full of concubines (*houri/ghilman*).

If and when they understand the concept of a deity-god is a misconception, because they fail to understand the One referenced as Allah in the Quran, they indulge completely in worldly and bodily pleasures, encouraging others to do the same.

On the other hand, imitators can also be found among humans.

Their religion, faith and the information they relay is all based on imitation. If you ask them to put aside the words of others and talk for themselves they'll have nothing to say. If they try, they'll probably contradict themselves, for an imitator's mental and intellectual capacity is underdeveloped. They live on a daily basis, unaware of the concept of life after death.

An imitator can't live alone; they are highly dependent on others. They are constantly in need of others' money, respect, esteem and attention…

A human of authenticity, however, is free of such needs. They are those who have found Allah in their essential reality and Allah is sufficient for them. Their sole purpose in life is to know Allah. Their only criterion is the Quran, whether they read it externally or internally; they base their life on the realities disclosed in the Quran alone.

An imitator lives to take; a person of authenticity lives to give.

An imitator wants to own; a person of authenticity loves to share.

An imitator spends his time with gossip; a person of authenticity spends his time attaining knowledge.

An imitator judges by surface value, their best skills are to criticize and insult others. A person of authenticity interacts with others only to share knowledge.

An imitator lacks tolerance; a person of authenticity is full of acceptance.

An imitator lives in his own cocoon world; a person of authenticity lives in THE world.

Salam be upon the people of authenticity…

30.1.99

NJ – USA

25

THE TRUTH HURTS

Sometimes the truth can be painful to hear, but it's imperative I share what I believe is true. The information I shared in *The Mystery of Man* in 1986, some of which I explore in more detail today, pertains to universal truths. Please take it seriously as it comprises the most important facets of life.

Those for whom money and sexuality are the central themes in life show interest in Sufism more as a hobby to comfort their conscience rather than to understand and experience its reality. They can never reach their purpose like this. They will only delude themselves and perhaps the people around them with the information they accumulate. This is indeed a serious responsibility.

Rumi recounts:

One day, Moses comes across a herd of sheep and a shepherd sitting under a tree talking to himself. He wonders what he's saying so he quietly listens. The shepherd says: "O my ALMIGHTY GOD! How I wish You were by my side right now, I would have loved You and hugged You, I would have fed You fresh milk, I would have laid You down on my lap and made You rest in the shade and I would have removed Your lice and nits and cut your nails…You are so beautiful, so gracious, so just… How would this world be without You? You watch us and see all that we do… We're going to come to Your presence in the future, please forgive our mistakes…! Please don't throw me into Your hellfire if I do wrong, please put me into Your heaven, I love You dearly but I can't see You, I wonder when I can see You…? My biggest desire is to come to Your presence and be with You, I'm willing to do whatever I can to earn Your favor, please forgive me if I can't obey all of Your commands…!"

It seems Moses not only had to deal with the Pharaoh, but also with shepherds…

So, what happened to that shepherd?

Well… today, he's the sheikh at the dervish lodge!

He's the *hodja* at the local mosque!

He's the professor at university!

Anyway, speaking of Moses (pbuh) and the Pharaoh…

Based on his knowledge of ancient scripts, the Pharaoh knew well there was no deity-god, and like his predecessors, he attributed his inherent godlike power to his identity-self, due to his lack of knowledge of the reality of Allah.

The Pharaoh was at the level of consciousness Sufism refers to as the *nafs-i mulhima* (the inspired self).

He saw himself as the One and all others as inexistent.

Everyone around him was his servant. They would observe all his commands without questioning.

His servants had no value for him. He would insult them, swear at them and degrade them at every chance. Lying to his servants and gossiping about them was permissible for him.

He would raise in rank those who exalted and respected him, and debase and discredit anyone who showed the slightest disrespect.

He did as he willed… Because he was the Pharaoh! The greatest!

Even the legendary Egyptian library, where he obtained all his knowledge from, meant nothing to him. He was the greatest, the one and only! His servants needed only to deify and worship him. He forbade them from performing salat or engaging in dhikr. He knew he was nothing without his servants, so he abhorred being alone. He taught some of his knowledge to some of his servants and let them also play god in his absence. His servants were like computers! Knowledge was no more than information in a database; their lives were based on earning and exercising power over others.

Lying and gossiping were permissible; nothing was considered wrong. Everyone lived to obtain something from others; it didn't matter how.

Knowledge was used merely as capital to earn and gain something.

When Moses disclosed the universal truths and warned the people, they attacked him.

Moses crossed the *Mulhima* sea with others who fulfilled the requisites of knowledge, while the Pharaoh tried to walk across the *Mulhima* sea with his servants.

Moses and the believers passed…

But the Pharaoh and his followers drowned and died in the *Mulhimah* sea, or shall I say, the Red Sea.

I will not be called to account for your deeds nor you for mine. Your deeds are of no concern to me and mine are of none to you. You to yourself, me to myself, each to themselves!

Take this knowledge I'm sharing with you and apply it in your life if it makes sense to you, leave others to themselves.

You're here to find Allah, if you have such an inclination. Wasting your time with the gossip of others will bring you nothing other than misery.

I wrote the *Power of Prayer* to explain that the most important thing in the world is prayer and dhikr. If you still don't grasp the importance of this then I have nothing further to say.

I wrote about the paramount importance of reading the prayers for protection, especially because those who engage in dhikr become more sensitive and hence more prone to direct or indirect contact with not only positive energy entities, but also, jinn. Taking advantage of this sensitivity, jinn make contact and prompt the ego, bringing out the pharaoh-like qualities in people under the guise of the *Mulhima* consciousness.

Some claim they trust Allah; therefore, they don't need to make such prayers. This is as ironic and contradictory as trusting the doctor, but not taking the prescribed medication.

Did the companions of the Rasul not trust him that they were so engaged in the prayers and verses he taught?

One who is devoid of knowledge and understanding can never discern the importance of the energy that is produced in one's consciousness, even when salat is not duly performed but attempted! Or how the dhikr of the Names of Allah aid in the development of the brain, even if one can't engage in contemplative dhikr.

Those who have fallen into the 'knowledge-trap' fail to see that becoming a Sufi knowledge-bank only aids in the growth of their ego because they don't continue reading the prayers for protection.

When those who take touristic trips to *Umrah* for entertainment or to comfort their conscience realize the loss they've accrued it will be too late to fix anything.

My friends…

Whoever tells you that performing salat is unnecessary and that dhikr is useless or discourages you from reading the prayers for protection, or lies, gossips or threatens, stay away from them, whoever they may be! Remember that Jesus was deceived by one of his closest companions!

The imitators will have no place near the people of authenticity in the afterlife!

Because those who can't cleanse themselves from the delusive concept of a deity-god and discern the reality of Allah fail to grasp the system, they wrongly think people will not face the consequences of their deeds – yet again falling into duality!

Whereas, the truth is, each will face the consequences of their own actions.

My friend…

If you lapse back into your delusions and relative conditioned rights and wrongs after true knowledge has come to you, you will not be able to pay the price and you will lead yourself straight to hell.

People can always make mistakes; if you follow them, you'll have your share in their mistakes.

My advice is, follow only the Rasul of Allah (saw) and the knowledge he disclosed instead of mortals like myself… Draw your own path with this knowledge, face the consequences of your own decisions and blame nobody.

May Allah protect us from pharaohs in the guise of sheiks and scholars, and secure us upon the way of Muhammad (saw).

25.1.99, NY-USA

26

TO KNOW OR NOT TO KNOW

It seems some still have trouble understanding that Islam is the name of the universal system comprising all forms and states of life in every dimension, functioning as part of a magnificent mechanism.

Those who realize this reality are the authentic ones. They are the ones who can evaluate the system. They are also those who have been deified in the past, or who are labeled as saint and friend of Allah today. Such eminent ones have known, found and become the reality within their own essence. Then they continued their lives on earth as humans until the end of their designated time.

The creator is Allah!

All of creation is in service to Allah.

Unbelievers squander their lives by disputing with the servants of Allah!

The warning of the Rasul (saw), "When two Muslims draw swords against each other, both the killer and the killed will go to hell," does not refer to a literal sword! Words and actions can sometimes be sharper than a sword, leading one to unimaginable suffering!

When even cats and dogs have owners, is it possible for a servant of Allah to not have an owner or a creator? But those who have not authenticated their faith cannot see this. For they are like computers, loaded with stories of Sufism and spirituality, and the ignorant are captivated by this information and believe them to be saints…

Some end up in hell because of their desire for fame or vengeance… And some stay clear from such inferior tendencies and end up in heaven…

One's tongue can lead one to hell or to heaven…

The people of the heart see the countenance of Allah wherever they look and speak only in this light, and thus go to heaven when they change dimensions…

But those who are too weak to strive with their own ego tend to be at strife with other egos in an attempt to satisfy themselves!

Others, who cleanse themselves by taming their egos, submit to Allah to the extent they are purified and spend their lives in strife based on the extent of their veil.

Man, on the other hand, reads the system and shares this knowledge.

Instead of spending his time in discord and rivalry, man strives to master and defeat his own egoistic tendencies.

Man knows the entire creation is created to fulfill a purpose, and the world is the plane by which the deeds of all people – the imitator and the person of authentication; the believer and the unbeliever; the intelligent and the unintelligent – will eventuate.

The unfortunate are those who, despite realizing the reality of the Rasul of Allah (saw), fail to gain insight from his teachings and choose to bicker and struggle with others rather than striving to tame their egos, most probably dying as unbelievers.

Consider the companions of the Rasul (saw) after he died and how they fell into conflict with one another…

We must understand the following hadith really well:

"Some of you will want to come next to me when I stand by the Pool of *Kawthar*, but the angels will prevent you. When I ask, 'They were my companions, where are you taking them?' They will reply, 'They did not follow your way; their place is hell.'"

After spending so many years in service to the Rasul of Allah (saw), if one fails to have tamed his ego and falls into the pit of dispute and strife, their place will not only be hell in the afterlife, but also in this world! This is inevitable. They will become so engulfed by the ambition to defeat one another they will place an inexhaustible abyss between themselves and Allah!

Mankind comes to this world alone, lives a large part of his life alone and will live completely alone in the life of the grave.

Think about how much of your life is spent in sleep, alone! And how much of your time is spent surrounded by crowds, yet alone! You might be surrounded by friends and family, but you're still alone. Despite this reality, you still don't prepare yourself for an infinite life to which you will travel… Alone!?

You'd have to take delight in horror and nightmare to not prepare yourself for a place where you will be completely alone…

My friends…

A hard disk full of data will not go to heaven! Remember, in the Quran, 'scholars' loaded with information who don't apply the requisites of this knowledge are likened to donkeys carrying books…

If we're not applying and experiencing our knowledge, then it is no more than a burden on our back.

As long as we're living, the door to repentance is open. It's never too late to mend, so long as we're not of the ungrateful…

If bodily and worldly pleasures are the central themes in one's life, then one is already damned. Why fill your heart with darkness and veil yourself from Allah by dealing and struggling with such energy fields? The more you interact with such people, the more you will become veiled from Allah and eventually lose faith.

While it was the duty of the Rasul of Allah (saw) to share the message, he did not enforce it upon anyone, so who are we to assume such roles? We did not come here to fight!

Abu Jahil ate and drank like the Rasul, and grew a beard like the Rasul, he dressed like the Rasul and walked like the Rasul, but he did not share his faith! Nor did/do all the others who will be taken away from the Rasul (saw) when he stands by the Pool of *Kawthar*.

If you don't want all your work to amount to nothing, take heed of the warnings of the Rasul, repent and realign yourself according to the principles of faith. Or have no doubt that what befell the deniers before you shall also befall you.

The system of Allah, the *sunnatullah*, will never change!

Every community upon which a calamity befell was warned beforehand. All those who were heedless enough to think they could rebel against the system of Allah faced severe consequences.

It is no use knowing the principles of faith, but not applying them in one's day-to-day life and relationships.

Lying, cheating and gossiping in the name of conciliation is a direct contradiction to faith and will lead one to die as an unbeliever even if he has spent his entire life praying and fasting. For such deeds are the direct result of denying Allah!

Please consider earnestly… Can one who has truly believed in Allah spend his time in gossip and the like? Such a faith is indeed questionable! Only the foolish can engage in such inferior activity.

Humans have been created for knowledge, and knowledge is what listens and knowledge is what talks! Where there is lack of knowledge there is rumors. Only one without belief will have plenty of gossip to do. And only the water of belief can extinguish the fire of gossip. Gossiping is such a provocative act that only those who seek the wrath of Allah will take part in it, lend an ear to it and resume it.

May Allah ease for us all the way of the Rasul (saw) through intellect and real faith.

19.2.99

New Jersey

27

WERE YOU NOT WARNED?

Oftentimes the truth can be disappointing… Sometimes one's parents, partner or best friend can cause the biggest disappointment. Nevertheless, it is only for an appointed time. Eventually, everything passes, life comes to an end and each goes their own way… You won't have to put up with anyone who doesn't share your system of thought or perspective in the eternal life. The togetherness here is only a physical one, whether they are your parents, children, partner or friend. And the self-interest, lying and deceit spawned from the idea of being the body are all bound to end in the hereafter. The hypocrisy and deceit based on material and bodily gain and pleasure will come to an inevitable end when one makes the transition to the next dimension of existence.

Neither one's possessions nor friends and relatives will be of any aid on that day.

Let's be clear about something… There are no gurus and masters here; we're not in the business of ego-training! We're sharing information, and it's up to each individual to take this information and use it for their advantage.

Having a master requires serious devotion and submission. Like Yunus Emre and his master Taktuk. Yunus' training took forty years! The ways of sainthood will not open without dedicating all of your time to a master and letting him train you, becoming imbued with the morals of Muhammad (saw) and making the act of giving your highest priority!

Acquiring Sufi knowledge does not render one a saint!

The same tool can both make or break a man.

One may use the internet to acquire Sufi knowledge and attain the secrets of the Quran; one may also use the internet to find a date!

Do not be deceived!

Recognize and discern the truth as though you've changed dimensions before you actually change dimensions, lest you become unimaginably disappointed. For on that day, nothing can console you, neither your acquisitions nor the people who stood by your side thinking you're a saint. Understand this well.

The knowledge in regards to Oneness, despite being the absolute truth, can actually be the means of constructing and strengthening the ego, for those who've not been trained. Those who have not been through the necessary training cannot duly comprehend the reality of Allah and the mechanics of the system, so with the knowledge of Oneness – and thus the realization of the invalidity of the concept of deity-god – they become very susceptible to using this knowledge in favor of their ego.

But one who lives solely for the sake of Allah cannot think about their bodily or material gain.

Nevertheless, an imitator cannot understand this.

Only a human is created for Allah.

A human has intellect; he lives for Allah.

An imitator is intelligent; he lives in pursuit of bodily and material gain and pleasures.

An intelligent imitator cannot evaluate the intellectual human; he surmises others to be like himself.

An unintellectual intelligent has a thinking capacity that is short-spanned and does whatever is necessary to gain worldly benefits and recognition.

An intellectual knows his immortality and lives only for Allah.

What the former plans to achieve is merely a tool for the latter, perhaps not even that.

Those who think judiciously about their selves should, for the sake of Allah, take a look in the mirror of the Rasul (saw). Not to see a beard and moustache, but to see his 'purpose'! How much do they share in common with the Rasul of Allah (saw)? What did he live for? What are they living for? How aligned can one's life be to that of the Rasul (saw), if one runs to fun and pleasure or sexual amusement at every opportunity?

One's androgen secretion flares up and prowls, the other has an estrogen rush and scours, another goes through andropause and treats himself to a supply of Viagra– yet all along talking of Sufism and spirituality solely to ease their conscience!

What will they find? Disappointment… Sooner or later…

My friends…

Let's face the truth. Let's discern the ephemerality of this world! Let's separate friend from foe, or shall I say, friend from the Antichrist!

Let's put aside our cookies and befriend one another for the sake of Allah!

Let's stop criticizing each other and begin to develop and move forward!

Allah created the system and informed us of the way it functions via the Rasuls. Those who can read it can inform those who can't read so they may at least believe and fulfill the requisites in order to save themselves.

It is because of the way this system functions that what I eat will not nourish you, and the medicine I take will not heal you!

The prayer and dhikr I practice will not be of any benefit to you. Each is to their own in this system. No one can pass on the reward of a practice you didn't engage in to you!

If you don't do dhikr, the specific advancements will not occur in your brain, regardless of who you know. If you don't read the prayers for protection in the Quran a hundred times a day, you will not be protected from the harmful beings that you can't perceive, despite who you know!

If you don't recite the prayer the Rasul of Allah (saw) read during Ascension,[14] there is a high chance you will unknowingly become subject to certain adverse influences. This is because the brain is unable to form the necessary field of protection as its capacity increases with

[14] Refer to *The Power of Prayer* for details.

dhikr, leaving you vulnerable to invisible beings. You may then succumb to their misguidance and fall far from Allah.

My friends, I write all of this with genuine intention and in your interest. I have no intention to criticize or hurt anyone's feelings. These are the truths I know. Allah be my witness, you will see the truth in my words in the future and you will be asked, "Were you not warned?"

Let us either fulfill the requisites of this knowledge upon the path of the Rasul (saw)… Or prepare ourselves for grave disappointment…

May Allah enable the comprehension of these truths…

12.2.99

Manhattan – NY, USA

28

FOR MY FRIENDS…

This is a letter for my future friends. If it reaches them, I hope they understand why I wasn't able to disclose certain things, or why I couldn't write more openly!

I'm compelled to be as careful and sensitive as one handling a newly laid egg.

How much can I disclose what I believe to be the truth under a governance that convicts one of supposedly holding an ill **'intention'** while reading a poem!?

How much of the realities referenced by the metaphors and symbols in the Quran can I reveal in a society that takes Islam as a religion sent down by a heavenly god?

How can I explain that, after I wrote about the nature of man's spirit being microwave rays produced by the brain in 1970, I was told by alleged Muslims, "microwaves are produced in an oven" – a short time after which the press confirmed there are innumerous microwave rays in the universe?

How can I tell those who think waves only consist of the FM radio waves that the brain actually receives and sends innumerous waves, the scope of which science is yet to figure out, and that life after death is also a world of such waves?

How can I explain to those who use religion for worldly gain and power that religion has nothing to do with worldly benefits?

How can I show those who think Allah is in space that there is no such deity-god concept and Allah exists with His Names in every iota of existence?

How can I explain that the Quran does not talk about a 'prophet' based on the understanding of a deity-god, but Nabis and Rasuls, based on the reality denoted by 'ALLAH'?

Or that when even the Rasul didn't have the authority to compel anyone to believe or practice anything no one has the right to enforce such things?

How can I explain that preventing young ladies who wear a scarf from attending educational institutions is a direct violation of universal human rights, freedom and democracy?

Or that religion is not a way of imitation and no one can advance an inch by imitating others?

Or that nobody except the Rasul of Allah (saw) should be followed; even if advice is taken from others, each person must determine their own path in life because there is no room for any excuse in the hereafter?

Or that the real weakness lies in the one that appears strong and hungry, and that the weak are bound to end up as bait, and of the grave results of passing on without being duly prepared?

How can I explain the system and order created by the One referenced as Allah is a conscious living being and what we call human, jinn, angel and satan are beings of the various dimensions of this mechanism?

How can I explain that nobody can be of any avail to one who doesn't fulfill the requisites of Islam disclosed by the Rasul of Allah (saw) in the hereafter? And that he will never have the chance to compensate for what he missed out on after death?

How can I explain the symbols and metaphors used in the Quran are manifestations sourced from the Risalah pertaining to the infinite aspect of man and the world?

Or that intercession is knowledge, and to reach intercession means to reach and apply knowledge, and to refuse intercession is to refuse the application of knowledge?

How can I explain that regardless of the age and century, the spirit of the Quran intends to prepare the people for the future, not to imprison them to the past, and to live by this spirit does not mean to change the

Quran? Or that those who fail to read the spirit of the Quran and take it literally will pay a grave price after death?

How can I explain that those who don't believe in the One whose name is Allah are actually in denial of their own essential qualities and because of this they can never experience the state of paradise?

Or that being a human means being a vicegerent and to live the requisites of this one must adopt a non-judgmental, objective and holistic approach at all times, and to evaluate things with the morals of Allah?

How can I explain that the topic that needs to be addressed with urgency is the cleansing of environmental and societal conditionings and the importance of adopting a universal viewpoint as free-thinking individuals?

How can I explain that, rather than marketing delusive and illusive concepts under the name of religion and using the capital of genuine Muslims to construct buildings and institutions, our first and foremost priority should be to unrequitedly spread true knowledge?

How can I explain to oppressors that there is no room for oppression in either the religion of Islam or the world of humanity?

Please try to understand me!

Ahmed Hulusi

11.10.98

Antalya

29

SCENARIO

Our house in New Jersey is not particularly large. It has two bedrooms upstairs. My office; one PC, two sofas and a library…

As I find the opportunity, I go downstairs to the lounge, which is as big as our bedroom in Turkey. Divided into two sections, one part is the dining area and the other part has a couple of sofas and my 53" TV.

Watching TV helps me rest my mind. As I work on my American accent, I observe their world of imagination…

There are mainly either soap operas full of emotional drama, or ultra-high-tech action movies. Sometimes I feel confused as I see the technology used in the movies and I think to myself, "How is it that these guys have such technology yet they can't cope with a single man like Saddam or Milosevic"

That's when one realizes that nothing is as it seems and a lot is going on in the background, and what is shown is very different to what is not shown!

That's when one realizes that anarchy, terrorism and war are intentionally and consciously not prevented, because certain people have vested interests, even though they have the power and means to stop these; they choose not to because of their personal gains! The arms industry is an important financial power, like the oil and gas industries! It's a world of those who sell and those who are bought out!

A world of elephants and mosquitos!

And then we write and condemn and protest… "Damn…!"

Sometimes I get carried away when I'm watching a movie, I start reacting, "What!? As if you would do that! You should have done this instead… What an idiot!" My wife, Cemile Kamer, looks at me and laughs, "This is how the scenario goes darling, if he doesn't do that how are the other events going to transpire? The poor man is only playing out his role, remember? Why are you getting mad at him? It's not his fault. Anyway, if he does what you think he should do then the movie can't progress this way. So, if you really want to be mad at someone, be mad at the screenwriter. Besides, aren't we all also playing the roles that have been written for us?"

When I'm warned like this from her highness I shut my mouth and sit back… I can't help but agree with her… For that moment!

The actor can't change the scenario!

Before heading back to my PC, I watch a little more NBC, FOX, CNN… I watch how many attacks have been launched against Bosnia, and listen how many more Bosnians have been slaughtered by the Serbs.

I hear about the number of deaths in Turkey and I feel sorry…

But this is "the reality of life!"

It's not a movie… Apparently!

We're born, we grow up. As we grow up, we adopt the values of our community, whether right or wrong, and become conditioned with them. We develop a character, with the added contribution of our genes of course, and thus begin the battle of life…

Sometimes we cheat, sometimes we're cheated; sometimes we wrong, sometimes we're wronged; sometimes we crush and rise, sometimes we break and rise, and sometimes, just to please our egos, we step on others and rise…

Some begin to think the world revolves around them, some think others will lose direction without their opinions!

Some of us battle for money, some for rank and recognition, and yet we all live for our country and for our people!

For the people we fill our pockets, for religion we fill our pockets, if not our pockets then our tags label rank and reputation!

What was the universal purpose of life?

Money…

Rank…

Fame…

Women…

All the games are played around these.

Everything is valuable until you attain it. It's valuable until you can buy it!

Once you can possess it, you lose interest; it's not that exciting anymore… Let's head for something new!

We think there's nothing that can't be bought or possessed or controlled!

"How much?" we continue to ask… We even attempt to appraise Allah!

There's never enough money!

Never enough rank!

Never enough fame!

Never enough women!

Because this is all we know!

And we don't have faith in the Rasul of Allah (saw), so why bother trying to reach the purpose he showed us?

We're only concerned about finding out more ways of eating, drinking and sleeping!

If it weren't for the fear of an illusory god, we wouldn't even give charity now and then or do any good for anyone.

Oh, but what if there *is* life after death?

This fear slows some of us down…

At least it restrains our animalistic tendencies… A little!

When the fear of fire and suffering joins the fear of god, it works like a brake! Those without such fears are like cars without brakes.

When do they stop? When they crash!

But all of this is just another stage of the play… We're not even aware! There are yet many stages being prepared for us!

Who you share this stage with, who you control, oppress or use and abuse in this stage is going to mean a great deal in the next stage… You're designing your seed, your spiritual genes right now… You have no idea what this seed is going to yield for you, what it's going to make you live!

The fathers eat the sour grapes, but the children's teeth are set on edge!

He who can't grasp the truth about life after death and direct his life accordingly, striving only for material gains and pleasures, will eventually be faced with great suffering.

Think about what the role you're playing now in this stage will lead to in the next stages; think about the consequences!

Even if you don't understand it, at least try to play a good role. If you can achieve this, you've been blessed. If you don't see the importance of this or don't feel the need to, then better prepare yourself for the suffering that will ensue!

I'm learning to take my wife's advice, I'm learning to see the screenwriter and not get mad at the actors…

Salam to you!

21.4.99

30

SOONER OR LATER

Once again, in the presence of each and every one of you, I'd like to confess my inability to duly thank my Rabb!

Science has finally proven the claim I made in 1985 and wrote in my book *The Mystery of Man* in 1986, that "the human brain is subject to various astrological effects and is programmed with cosmic rays coming from the sun and other planets in our solar system"!

Indeed, there is no god in space with a pen in his hand, writing on the wrinkles and folds of our brain!

It's not possible for those who can't rid themselves of the idea of a god in space to read the system that Islam talks about... Perhaps they're compelled to be imitators.

Let's see how science is validating the things I wrote 14 years ago.

This is what Engin Ardic wrote about in *Star Newspaper* on April 11, 1999:

Maurice Cottorell, an electrical engineer and writer, was a little skeptical when examining the Van Allen Belts surrounding the earth's atmosphere. He realized the Van Allen Belts, discovered by James Van Allen in 1957 while working for NASA, absorbed the sun's radiation and sent it to the earth and the sun sent 12 different types of rays during a one year cycle, which created 12 different magnetic fields (these magnetic fields were discovered by British astronomer Iain Nicolson).

Twelve... Cottorell suddenly had an epiphany... The star signs are also 12 in total he thought, 12 signs associated with 12 months and 12 different magnetic fields. There's something more to this!

After extensive research, Cottorell came across the works of Prof. A. Lieboff from Oakland University. In an experiment he conducted, Prof

Lieboff found that the lighting arrangement in his laboratory had various effects on fetal cells growing in test tubes.

Based on this data, Cottorell claimed the 12 different sun rays lead to 12 different mutations in the fetal chromosomes (whether the fetus is in a test tube or in the mother's womb) resulting in 12 different types of personalities.

And thus, the star signs!

He loaded this data into his computer and looked for correlations between certain wavelengths, sun-spots, birth dates and the behavioral effects on people. The computer verified his claim. If a fetus was conceived during the formation of a sun-spot (radiation blast), it resulted in a specific character type.

This finding was like a key unlocking an enormous castle of hidden knowledge!

I believe, in the future, this door is going to be opened even wider and many of my claims are going to be verified as true. Just as an aside, I wonder if they will ever question how it was possible that Ahmed Hulusi had written about this years before it was scientifically proven?!

What matters for now is that it has been verified that cosmic rays of the sun affect the genes, leading to specific types of mutations. At later stages, they're going to discover that it is not only the sun, but all of the planets in the solar system that have similar effects.

And it's not just about the point of conception, but also the 120th day after conception and the moment of birth that play important roles in terms of the programs that are received.

Sooner or later!

But slowly… Perhaps after I change dimensions! I'm 54, who knows how much longer I will live…?

Yes my friends…

I've explained the system I've 'read' to the best of my capacity. If you understand this system well, you'll realize there is no deity-god in space and all the practices recommended by Islam are for your own good, as per the necessity of the system.

You'll see that the teachings of Muhammad (saw) have nothing to do with the Islam that is being preached today. And you'll feel the need to prepare for your life after death and refrain from wasting your time on things that are not going to mean anything for you tomorrow.

Know well that true peace is only possible by ending the wars in the world and understanding the reality of Islam.

If we want our problems to end, we must cleanse ourselves from the misconceived and misconstrued 'Muslimism' and allow ourselves to experience the ease of the essence of Islam.

Let us try to get to know Muhammad, the Rasul of Allah (saw), leaving aside the thousand-year-old misconceptions with which we've been indoctrinated.

Thank you, Engin Ardic, for making this information available to us.

Thank you, my Rabb, for confirming my statement after 14 years.

11.4.99

31

THE QUANTUM DIMENSION AND THE GENES

He recorded the Quran in the organic memory of his mind, and he re-played it over and over again. Thus, they called him a hafiz.

Though he re-played it endlessly, he never actually READ it. Let alone the entire text, he hadn't even read any of its verses. Perhaps he didn't know it was meant to be read, perhaps he didn't know how...

We live in an interregnum in which memorizers and conveyors are considered scholars, and those who narrate fairy tales and stories are considered saints!

I try to elucidate a topic and I'm faced with the ludicrous cliché defense, "But there is such and such verse in the Quran and such and such hadith that claims such and such!"

These expressions are desperate attempts made by memorizer brains, devoid of the ability to contemplate, in the name of defending their memorized and conditioned data! I doubt they ever gave those verses a serious thought to really grasp their meaning and understand their purpose of revelation. Such examples are like sheep waiting to be shepherded. They ask, "Okay okay, just tell me, what shall I do now?"

Go and graze on grass for god's sake, I don't know!

If you had the capacity to read the Quran, you would know what to do!

Then they ask, "When can we see you?"

Never!

If you can't read my writings, how can you see 'me'?

What benefit is there in seeing my appearance if you can't use your brain and contemplate?

I say, "What you're seeking is within you."

They say, "How about we see you?"

I'm within you!

I *am* you!

How much longer are you going to search outside?

Ingratitude...

This word describes those who don't know the value of what they've been given.

The biggest punishment for an ungrateful one is the end of blessings. And the only cause of this is the person himself. The ungrateful one causes harm to himself.

The ungrateful ones who don't evaluate knowledge punish themselves by allowing themselves to be deprived of knowledge forever.

The Quran is the biggest blessing to us, from the Rasul of Allah (saw). Repeating the Quran without thinking about its meaning, and without entering and exploring the vast universe contained within it, is ungratefulness. The Quran is the sublime book that has been disclosed to man, the vicegerent, to expound the universal secrets.

But alas... You still think you're a sack of flesh and bones, and squander your life with topics related to this puny sack! But such is life; those who wish are free to turn their eternal lives into hell should they choose to!

Man is beyond the boundaries of time and space!

The life of the flesh-bone human is like a mere flash in the galactic dimension of time, but how about after that? Where and how will it be?

What does the Quran say about this?

> **"Subhan is He who created all pairs** (DNA helix) **from what the earth** (body) **produces and from themselves** (their consciousness) **and from that which they don't know!"**[15]

> **"And a sign for them are the ships We carried full with their progeny!"**[16]

> **"It is He who created the pairs** (double helix DNA) **and formed ships** (consciousness) **and animals** (biological body) **upon which you ride."**[17]

> **"And We created everything in pairs** (positive – negative energy; the double stranded DNA)**... That perhaps you will remember and contemplate."**[18]

I talked a little about quantum physics and the holographic make-up of the universe in *The Observing One* (1995) and *Spirit Man Jinn* (1970). I tried to explain how the Quran alludes to these realities.

Every particle at the quantum level, the essence of the material world, exists with its pair.

Let's remember the word Allah is a name, a reference. As the verse "It was Allah who threw" is essentially a reference to everything, as everything is composed of the same 'stuff', whatever its level of existence may be. Thus, the word Allah points to the materialized form of existence, appearing as 'many,' as much as it points to the 'oneness' that can be observed at the quantum level.

But of course, having said all of this, it is also imperative to remember that Allah is beyond all of this and totally free from being confined to or limited by any form or concept.

The station referred to as the Spirit or the Grand Spirit in Sufism is in fact the quantum dimension, an indivisible field of oneness, which comprises the essence of all perceivable and unperceivable things. Consciousness at this level "manifests anew at every instant" due to the various interactions of the quants.

---

[15] Quran 36:36
[16] Quran 36:41
[17] Quran 43:12
[18] Quran 51:49

All quants exist as pairs and are perceived as either photons or waves, and they are constantly in communication with one another, even if the other is on the other side of the galaxy!

The quants of the quantum universe are like the genes of the animal life (the body life). The genes are symbolized as "ships" in the Quran; ships that carry certain meanings from the quantum dimension to the level of matter. They are space ships that carry travelers of meaning from the quantum space to the plane of matter at the speed of light. Genes that exist as pairs form our livestock-vehicles, i.e. our bodies, and the chromosomes sail in the cytoplasm of the cell like ships.

At the quantum level, everything exists as a single consciousness. This single unified field of consciousness is called the First Intellect in Sufism. The quantum level is the attribute of life itself!

All of the angels in existence have been formed from this single angel, also called the Spirit, or the quantum level that comprises the essence of all of us.

In other words, the angelic dimensions formed from this quantum field of oneness create all the perceivable and unperceivable things.

Essentially, everything is just an observation; it is the quantum level observing itself!

Time and space do not apply to this plane.

If and when man completes his journey to his essential reality, the 'constructed person' or ego-identity will become annihilated and only the Self will remain to observe its Self!

7.7.99

32

TIME

A serious intruder!

It has crudely invaded our world!

It took over our minds and locked down our thought system; it controls our thoughts…

Time!

We mortals have made time the commander of our thoughts. We can't think without it! We can't even imagine life without it!

The most we can do is rant on about how "time is relative, and time doesn't really exist" and so on… Rather like grey parrots…

I'm this age at this time… Which time??!!

How much of the truth pertaining to the state beyond the flesh can you expect from one who lives in the state of the flesh and thinks with the flesh?

They buy flesh, sell flesh, chase after flesh! They think of man as flesh and live for flesh! They judge man according to his flesh and then confine him to the limits of 'time'!

And we still ask… "When???"

The Rasul of Allah (saw) talked about the coming of events… He said days will come when women will dress like men and style their hair like camel humps… 1400 years ago! But he didn't give a specific time… He spoke of many signs of Doomsday, but he didn't give specific time to any of them…

Many enlightened ones have also talked about future events, but none of them specified the time…

Why is this so?

Because the concept of time doesn't exist in the state of those who live beyond the flesh! They perceive and experience these realities in a state beyond the flesh!

If, out of our persistence, they specify a time, they will probably be mistaken. For it is misleading to construe that which is timeless, with time.

Events may be observed and experienced in timelessness, like waves one after another... Or like dreams, seen one after another...

Even though there is some sense of time in a dream, it is entirely due to the already existing data in one's brain; it's not real! Hence, it isn't possible to say exactly when something will transpire, based on a dream... One may assume the coming of an event based on a dream, but one cannot determine when it will happen.

This reality is a little different for the enlightened ones among the followers of the Rasul of Allah (saw). Their perception doesn't even need vision, like that in a dream, as they are said to be able to perceive and sense the coming of an event based solely on their instincts and the manifestation of this in their comprehension. For their state of reality is pure consciousness, free from the concepts of time and space. Beneath this state is another state, one in which visions during the awake state occur, similar to the dream state.

Perceiving without vision is called revelation in the case of Rasuls, and inspiration in the case of his followers... Realities that are perceived in this state do not appear in any particular 'form', hence the concept of time is inapplicable to them.

They say such beings experience life in a totally different way to our flesh-based world! As though they travel through timelessness and formlessness mounted on a *Buraq* or a *Rafraf* while discovering what they discover in their own consciousness (in reality *Rafraf* refers to the ability to detach from the body and bodily limitations and *Buraq* is the ability to appear at any place at any time at the speed of thought.)

Then they deign to our level of flesh... While some appear as flesh and articulate their observations, the novice tries to conceptualize existence within the boundaries of time... But time frames are for the level of flesh, they're open to misunderstandings and misjudgments...

It would be great misfortune for us to misevaluate these realities, we'd be reducing and confining ourselves to the level of flesh if we do…

Man has been created in a realm of timelessness and spacelessness. He can't even be considered to be a spirit at this level of existence, yet his very existence has a spirit and it is the necessity of this spirit that he searches for his essence, his essential self, so that he may find true peace.

One who is created from earth will run after earthly pleasures and eventually return to earth…

One who is created from this dimension will spend his life in longing and eventually return to his home…

Everything will return to its essence!

5.4.99

NJ – USA

33

DON'T TOUCH THIS BOOK WITHOUT PURIFYING YOURSELF FIRST

If you read it literally, without heeding the verse, "We explain to you with metaphors", the Quran talks about bodies made of earth, a place called hell full of fire, gardens full of all sorts of fruits and companions (*houris*), and a god with a hand who watches us from above…

Oh and of course *barzakh* (the Intermediary Realm) and Doomsday, and a day when the earth will become flat like a big tray and all the people will gather upon it…

And stars that fall and set in space, and angels holding and carrying hell, while it boils under the tray-like earth and guards who carry the people to giant scales to weigh their good deeds against their bad deeds… Would've thought they'd opt for electronic scales by now?!

After the mass weighing of billions and billions of people, a giant bridge will be made from the earth to the big garden called paradise going over the flames of hell… The circumference of the earth that the flames surround will be millions of kilometers long.

The chief of staff will apparently call out "follow what you idolize and deify" and everybody will begin to follow the idol they worshipped in the world. When the idol comes to the bridge it'll fall over into the flames below, and its followers will fall after it!

Those who didn't worship any particular idol and prostrated to Allah, on the other hand, will wait in their spots until they hear the call, "Follow the Rasul or Nabi you followed in the world". They then will follow their Rasul or Nabi, and come to the Bridge of *Sirat*. Some will pass at lightning speed and some will pass limping and crawling, until they reach the gardens called paradise!

In short, this is the 'literal' explanation of the life awaiting us after death in the Quran.

Does the night of ascension refer to a trip where the Prophet went to space and met god?

Is salat about placing your head repeatedly in the sand?

Why has salat has been reduced to a form of exercise, and the imam to a personal trainer?

"The greatest losers among humanity are those who don't perform prostration (*sujud*) and bowing (*ruku*) as they deserve to be performed..."

What is the true meaning of prostration? Is it to place your forehead on the ground for a really long time?

For man to come to grips with how little he knows, he first needs knowledge.

The Quran is the book of knowledge!

The Rasul of Allah (saw) is an integral and faultless inviter to the reality with revelation and universal knowledge that has become manifest in his perception.

This book of knowledge claims there is no god or godhood, only Allah!

But it is not possible for those who haven't cleansed themselves from the idea of a deity/god to fathom this!

The Quran, from beginning to end, gives guidance to man by denouncing the concept of a deity-god.

The Quran is NUR!

It is light!

It sheds light to brains that have been left in darkness, to show them the reality!

How can the Quran be valid until Doomsday?

With outdated beliefs of celestial gods?

Or by claiming the one up there is writing the scenario?

Or by decoding the codes and metaphors he used?

The secret is hidden in the warning, "We explained all things in metaphors."

If we can't put to use this hint, we'll begin to contrive absurd ideas and end up in hell without having benefited from the timeless Book of Knowledge and discovering the endless potential comprising our essence.

The Rasul of Allah (saw), the discloser the Quran, says, "When you're *invited* to salat…"

We are *invited* to read the Book at least five times a day!

Why can't salat be without ablution? What is ablution? How is it made?

Why can't salat be without the *Fatiha*?

I wonder if we're aware?

The muezzin… To what is he calling the people with the *adhan*? Is he conscious of the invitation he's making?

Are the people conscious and aware of what they're being invited to?

How are we to purify ourselves and take ablution to attend the muezzin's invitation?

As I explained in *The Power of Prayer*, the Rasul of Allah (saw) advises that we read a prayer that begins with the line, "O Allah, the Rabb of this complete invitation…" after the *adhan*… Why 'complete' invitation? To what is it a complete invitation?

What is the muezzin inviting us to?

Could it be to the experience of ascension?

Is salat not the ascension of the believer?

Understand that the call for prayer is essentially a call for ascension!

Abdulqadir al-Jinali says, one who doesn't experience ascension isn't performing salat!

But ascension is the tool, the means to experience something else.

What is it that we're actually being invited to experience, I wonder?

And why was this invitation intended to be compulsory 50 times a day?

Did you ever think of the call to prayer as an invitation to live an ascension to your higher reality?

How is the call to prayer recited?

Who hears it? Who perceives it? Who responds to it?

Why is salat a compulsory practice for the believers?

Why at least five times a day?

What are those who don't respond to this call missing out on?

It's as though ears have become deaf!

Has Doomsday started or what?

The sun has darkened, i.e. knowledge has faded, and the stars have fallen, i.e. the people of knowledge have retreated…

The world has become crammed with those who are blind to the reality and deaf to the *adhan*, and impotent from speaking the truth!

Man has become silenced!

Only the tape recorders are playing, repeating their memorized knowledge over and over again…

Help us, O Allah!

19.7.99

34

HIM and I

One size bigger… But very different to what we can fathom!

Its size is beyond our comprehension!

It's so big that its infinite!

Such a mighty body! It's so deep that it's limitless!

As if it has a million heads, billions of arms, trillions of legs!

The organs of its body are the billions of galaxies!

The cells of its organs are the hundreds of billions of stars!

The cell sequences are the constellations of stars!

That giant body has awareness, just like we do.

It has a sense of 'I' or 'I am' just like we have an ego-identity!

It has consciousness, just like we do! It's aware of its own existence and its essential nothingness, just like we are also aware of our nothingness at the core essential level.

It's infinite and limitless, its name is Universe! Infinity and illimitability are merely relative concepts for creation!

I am infinite, eternal; my name is Human!

It's created; its name is Spirit!

I'm created; my name is Human…

Its organs are renewed, its body is renewed, supernova blasts take place, and then they're replaced by new ones! Ad infinitum…

My organs are also renewed, my body is renewed, my cells blast, they die, and then they're replaced by new ones!

Its body has a spirit, that holds its body up! Its Spirit is conscious; it organizes the system!

My body has genes; it organizes my body and manifests my spirit.

I travel in it, to it, with it!

It observes me, through me, with me!

I ascend to my heaven…

To my heart, my spirit, my secret, the hidden treasures of the Divine Names and Attributes within my consciousness??

Man becomes nothing, It becomes everything… The observed and the Observer!

My self (*nafs*) thinks with my heart.

It watches the Names with my Spirit.

It says "Only I exist!" and the hearer of the call is itself!

Shhh… Stop there and be quiet!

It's the universe, the worlds, the angel called Spirit!

It also has a Self (*nafs*).

It also has a heart.

It also has a spirit.

It also has a secret.

It also has a *hafi* (hidden). And an *ahfa* (most hidden).

The point…

The point is the universe… The point in the universe, is me!

The point, is created…

I'm nothing at the point, impoverished, wretched, impotent and in need!

The point does dhikr to the Creator, with its billions of organs and hundreds of billions of tongues…

I do dhikr to my creator, with every single one of my trillions of cells, at every instant!

With the tongue of each of my cells, with the tongue of each of my organs, with the tongue of my spirit, my consciousness, and the meaning of my existence…

The world is doing dhikr, the worlds are doing dhikr…

The world is doing tasbih, the worlds are doing tasbih…

The point is turning, around its own purpose of creation.

All points are turning around the point of their purpose of creation…

Everything is turning, around ONE thing!

There is an angel called SPIRIT.

Then there are angels, created from that angel, and more angels created from other angels!

There are angels, sublime… There are angels, veiled… Angels, veiled from their own observation of angelic qualities!

Angels are Nur!

Angels are consciousness!

Angels are *gayyur* (jealous)!

An angel becomes one creature at one point, and another creature at another point!

They play among each other! Wheels of fortune are turning in the universe!

All angels serve their purpose of creation…

Those that are named devils… And those that are named humans, though some of us are a little like this or a little like that according to others of us!

Some of us are oceans, some of us are mere drops in the ocean… But we're all in the same boat, at the end of the day… Going to some unknown town!

The end of existence is inexistence.

The end of hell is nothingness.

The life of a point is exhaustion.

Allah is al-GHANI!

ALLAH IS HU!

35

INSIDE OR OUTSIDE?

"When I look at you I know Doomsday is near!" my grandmother Cenan would say to me…

When she married the postmaster of Mecca and gave birth to my mother Adalet, her fourth daughter, in Mecca, my mother was placed on the doorsill of the Kaba, as was the custom, and prayers were made that she be a righteous person… Grandma would narrate this story frequently…

Apparently, her father had disputed with Sayyid Hasan Efendy, then Amir of Mecca, endangering our whole family history and lineage! He stood up against him and said, "Sufficient for me is the knowledge of Allah, you mean nothing to me!"… After which, they moved to Turkey and assumed the surname "Yesilbag," which means "green tie," as it was custom in those days for the sayyid to tie a green tie around their heads…

Hence, grandma would liken me to her father, who nearly demolished our entire lineage when he was upset! She'd get exasperated from my (the atheist child raised in Istanbul!) obscure questions, and say, "This boy is a sign that Doomsday is upon us!"… When she passed away during her 80s, I was only 17, and with a sudden turn, I started reciting the call to prayer at Cerrahpasha Mosque across the street from our house in Istanbul!

I tried fervently to awaken the people to the reality, and on many occasions, was insulted and sworn at… Nevertheless, for my grandma, I was the sign of Doomsday… That's the image she had of me when she left this realm…

Obviously, for someone who was born almost a century ago and spent most of her life in Mecca, a child of Istanbul born in 1945 was rather complicated and confusing, and thus a sign of the nearing of Doomsday…

Whereas now, when I look at the way the youth talk and their areas of interest, I can't help but look at *them* as signs of Doomsday!

After nearly 40 years of extensive research and study, I still find it difficult explaining some of these topics to my peers, let alone to teenagers, who not only comprehend things quickly, but challenge me with such daring questions that, while trying to answer them, I find myself thinking "Signs of Doomsday, these kids!"

As it turns out, these "signs of Doomsday" are quite cognitive! They grasp quickly the fact there is no god in space, especially if they haven't been raised in a conservative family.

They understand there is no "god," but when it comes to understanding and experiencing the reality denoted by Allah, things go a little haywire…

They understand at an intellectual level the size of the universe, but when it comes to understanding its dimensionality, they get confused…

My book *Allah* became quite popular on the internet recently. Among its readers is Bill Donahue, a researcher from New Jersey. Recently, four or five of the 45 minute shows he hosts every week has been about my book *Allah*. He's around my age, maybe a little older. It's worth seeing how he explains the invalidity of the concept of godhood and the reality that only Allah exists (https://www.youtube.com/watch?v=tQKacYNfIdk).

Though this is where it gets a little complicated… Bill says, "God isn't in space. He's *inside* us!"

Just like our nouveau Sufis!

Allah isn't inside us! He isn't *inside*!

Allah is AHAD and SAMAD!

Concepts such as 'inside' and 'outside' do not apply to Him. He is beyond concepts such as 'me' or 'you.' You can't conceive Him to be inside yourself. If you do, you're creating another god and calling him Allah. Allah isn't a god. He is bereft, he is al-Ghani. But knowing this isn't sufficient. One needs to feel and experience this.

Narrating from Zen teachings Bill says, "If you die before you die then you won't die when you die" and explains the only way to know one's self is to abandon the concept of god and understand Allah, frequently using the word 'inside' as a reference.

But where is this *inside*?

When we say inside, what exactly do we have in mind?

Are we talking about an individual inside or a collective one?

Both are incorrect. Remember Allah is AHAD.

Concepts such as inside and outside are relative terms; they exist only for creation. The Absolute Reality is AHAD and SAMAD. Every quality or attribute that comes to mind is obsolete in the sight of His *Ahadiyyah* (the Absolute Oneness of existence). He is beyond all conceptualized ideas and thoughts.

When He observes Himself on you, you will no longer be. Therefore, your inside won't exist either. Even the idea of an inside will disappear.

Allah is such Oneness that none other has ever existed and will ever exist!

He is beyond the concepts of inner and outer, and His Oneness renders all gods and concepts of godhood invalid and inexistent.

As for 'me'... 'I' am merely an assumed reality who is essentially inexistent... An inexistent servant of Allah...

1.4.99

New Jersey - USA

36

R.I.P.

The real world outside your cocoon…

The concepts of the real world…

Realistic values on which these concepts rest…

The world of dreams and assumptions inside the cocoon world…

The concepts of your world…

And yet another layer thickening your cocoon weaved with your value judgments constructing your concepts…

Yesterday is a dream today… Past and gone…

Today is going to be a dream tomorrow…

You're going to be in another world tomorrow, a world built on the foundation of today!

Yesterday you cried…

Yesterday you laughed…

Yesterday you got angry and frustrated…

Yesterday you were joyful and happy…

If you're living in the now today, everything you experienced in the past will only make you laugh today…

But still, realize that everything you're living right now is the direct result of the things you lived in the past!

If you're unhappy, look at your past… Don't blame anyone but yourself!

Do you really think by repeating "*La ilaha illallah*" or "Allah" or reciting *surah al-Ikhlas* 40 thousand or 100 thousand times guarantees your place in paradise?

You're merely repeating these words! If you had experienced their meaning just once, the only thing preventing you from going to paradise now would have been your body.

Perhaps you placed your forehead on the ground countless times, but you never once consciously experienced the reality of prostration.

Perhaps you fasted numerous times, but never once stopped being a cannibal!

While your tongue proclaimed Allah, your lifestyle exposed something else.

So, what kind of a future are you actually expecting?

Your entire life is a gamble! You're veiling yourself from the reality with your own hands!

It has been narrated that, after reaching the age of 40, if one still hasn't turned to Allah, the Satan sits on his head, swings his legs downwards to cover his eyes and claims "I've taken this person as my captive, he is my slave from now on!"

Expect your return from whom you serve, not from anyone else! Don't fool yourself again!

The return you're getting today is the result of your servitude. Great if you're happy. But if you're not, then know that your service is misdirected!

You haven't died yet!

So, come and repent before your last breath and turn to the creator of the heavens and the earth (levels of consciousness and body) from within your depths…

My friend… You say "Is this what I deserve, is this what I'm worth?"

Let me give you the key to the system and order of Allah with which you can leave your cocoon…

Your worth is defined by nothing but the result of your own doings!

What you deserve is the purpose for which you have been created, determined before your birth.

Whatever an individual needs to reach his creational purpose is what he deserves, in the real sense.

These may come to you either as grants or through divine deceit.

If you become deceived, that is, if you don't recognize the scheme and fall for it, you'll suffer in the end.

You'll cause yourself to become deaf and blind to the truth and render your consciousness incapable of functioning, after which, nothing will be of avail…

So be thankful if you can see your inadequacy now, and make a change.

Know that, underneath all mistakes lies an insufficient or incorrect understanding of the system and order, an understanding based on the concept of 'god' or godhood. In other words, a world full of wishful thinking… Far from the reality.

Again, if you want to see what you deserve and what you're worth, look at your lifestyle.

Don't deceive yourself!

When you commence your life in the plane of the spirit, you're going to be imprisoned in the building you're constructing right now!

You'd be wise to construct one in which you can *rest in peace*!

37

HOW MANY COOKIES DO YOU HAVE IN YOUR CLOSET?

They ask me "How many cookies do you have in your closet?" … Come to think of it, quite a few!

How about you?

I've made so many cookie-deities out of my value judgments that I've lost count!

I don't know how many times I created a judgment-cookie and deified it for some time before I got over it and ate it!

I wonder how many times my environmental conditioning and the brainwashing to which I was subject caused me to make cookie-idols and become a slave to them!

Perhaps we don't even realize how we prostrate to the cookie-idols we create!

I had found it ridiculously funny when I had read about how Omar (ra) would make cookie idols before going on a trip, then he'd worship them and then when he got hungry he would eat them!

I spoke too soon!

I was astonished to see how much I was doing the same thing while thinking I was practicing the principles of Islam!

Everything from my sleep, to my fasting and prostration, from my thoughts to my discussions was filled with cookie-idols, and I wasn't even aware!

We have so many cookie idols… Some we can't even spare, and others we can't give up and carry around, just for the sake of it!

If we can't abandon these cookies during our lifetime, what's going to happen when we crossover?

Will death do us apart?

Or will we be buried with them, like the pharaohs?

Know, my friend, talking about the truth won't get you to the truth!

You're going to be on your own in the afterlife, if you're smart, pull yourself together and call yourself to account now!

Realize your cookie-idols and abandon them! You've memorized it well to say, "He's not out there, He's in here!" but where's *in here*?

Take a moment to reflect on the word "inside" …

Where exactly is "inside"?

Is it inside your head?

Or inside your brain?

Is it inside your cells and atoms?

Perhaps it's inside your spirit?

Or inside your Nur if you have any…?

Who's the one saying *inside* in the first place?

What's inside?

Where's outside?

The inside of your outside, or the outside of your inside!?

Are *you* outside and inside? Or inside and outside, you?

Feel your self, what kind of a self are you?

While observing my faults during the Mercury retrograde, I'm watching the One manifesting Itself as me through the Pluto-Chiron conjunction… My consciousness has become silenced!

May Allah help us to recognize our cookie-idols and be cleansed of them.

25.3.99

38

THE POWER OF THE COOKIE

Did you ever wonder from where the cookie-gods derive their power?

Why do so many people light candles in temples and give offerings to their gods from whom they apparently receive answers? How is it that their prayers and wishes come true?

Is Allah deceiving them with divine deception (*makr*)?

Remember the 'inner' is hidden on the 'outer', the *Safiyah* (the Pure Self) is hidden in the *Ammarah* (the Inciting Self) and takes the shape and color of its container, and that all layers are essentially a single layer, and *al-Ghani* manifests according to the shape and form of the 'outer'…

Even though sunlight is a single color yet becomes multiple colors through a prism, the Pure becomes different through the sub-conscious…

Electricity is seen as the color of the lamp…

Thus, when a person goes to their temple or god and asks for something… Who's actually responding to the prayers of these people?

Not from outside, but from you! Everything that transpires from you is derived from 'you'!

Allah does not interfere from the outside… It's manifesting from your own essence… The decree of Allah…

If you can't succeed, look for the reason in your self! If you really want somcthing with all your heart, nothing can stop it from happening other than divine determination.

Thus, the power in the cookie-idol is no other than the creative power of Allah in you!

You focus on something, you believe it's going to happen, you put all your effort into this particular desire, and then it happens.

Is it the cookie-god that made it happen? Is it the candle you lit, the rag you tied on a wishing tree, the offering you made? Or is it you?

The world is nothing but a stage play in which you are the main character.

According to your values, you are always honest, but others aren't!

You become veiled with your assumed relative values because of the limitation of your comprehension, but a day will come and you'll be astonished to see your mistakes and shortcomings…

You won't ever question yourself, you'll only ask "why is this person doing this to me? Why is this person treating me this way?" and judge others based on their external behavior, justifying the situation and rendering yourself innocent.

But the reality is, you attracted that person to yourself to reflect your own unfavorable behavior!

Perhaps an eclipse happened in your consciousness and you made a misevaluation in the dark and thus encountered this result!

Could the advice, "Seek what you seek within yourself, everything is in you!" be pointing to the reality that 'you are a co-creator'!?

If you're the main character in your play and living your own fate, and you're inviting the things you're living with what you're resonating from your 'inner'… And you *choose* to worship the cookie-idols you create, then to whom can you complain when the cookies hurt your teeth or give you a tummy ache?

You're the main character of your own play! When the play ends, you're going to leave the stage alone, and go home on your own, everything you supposedly own on the stage is going to remain on the stage!

The only reason you're in this world is to train and develop yourself, not to bake and eat cookies! Stop deifying worldly possessions and pleasures, my friend!

If you're about to drown and someone reaches out to you, will you not unquestionably hold their hand? If you want to be saved, you'll hold the hand that reaches out, whether you like them or not.

When one is young, he's usually hot tempered and unable to think calmly and objectively. And when one is old, he loses his reason and feels unable to detach from all the things he possessed and became attached to during his life… He loses his ability to reason and evaluate, he forgets the purpose of his life and begins to bicker and quarrel!

But one who chooses falsity has chosen it himself and if this is what has been created for, you can't do anything to change that!

The Rasuls and their followers never quarrel or argue with anyone. For, they know that whatever purpose a person has been created for, that is going to be made easy for them, and that is the path they're going to choose! Hence, the Rasuls and their followers are only concerned about sharing the message, not trying to convince anyone!

But of course, there have always been and will always be those who share this knowledge for worldly pursuits…

Let us know my friends that we have been created for Allah!

Let us stop our wishful cookie thinking and realize the reality of our selves, and live accordingly!

Our friend is one who channels and guides us to our essence!

Our enemy is one who pulls us to the struggle of multiplicity and encourages us to spend our lives in gossip and quarrels.

How much of your time each day do you spend for your main and essential purpose? And how much of your time each day do you spend in pursuit of things that are going to have absolutely no meaning and no benefit to you in the next life?

Let me repeat. The power of the cookie comes from the force of your belief!

Instead of using that force on the cookie, use it to reach your actual purpose so that you inherit the kingdom of the heavens!

Believe in Allah, the One in your essence, and live accordingly!

2.3.99

39

WHERE ARE YOU HEADING?

Are we aware, my friend, of where we've come from, and where we're going?

Some may say, "Sure... after a brief experience of earthly life we're all going to go on to the afterlife..."

Some may say, "Why of course! We came from Allah and to Allah we shall return!" just as they've heard or read...

But where is Allah? Does Allah have a location from which we departed and to which we will return?

Isn't this the outlook of a deity-centric understanding?

Did we really contemplate how we came from Allah?

According to the intimates of reality, at every instance, we come into existence from nothingness and become inexistent the next instant, then come back into existence the instant after, and become inexistent again the next instant, ad infinitum...

So, where exactly are we coming from and where are we going?

From nothingness to nothingness, you say?

As far as I'm concerned, with all this excess baggage of existence, I don't think we're going anywhere near nothingness, despite coming from it... It seems we are unable to leave our precious world behind!

But the Rasul of Allah (saw) says, "The world and everything in it will be cast into hell. The world and everyone who is attached to it have been created for hell!"

It seems to be a good idea to rid ourselves of the world!

Blessed are those who have no possession...

Neither worldly, nor of their 'self'!

But where is this 'self' coming from in the first place?

What's the path?

The intimates of reality have made a classification encompassing the body, self, heart, spirit, secret, and the hidden treasures of the Names and Attributes…

And they talked about the levels of consciousness or the layers of the self as:

Nafs-i Ammarah: The Inciting Self

Nafs-i Lawwama: The Self-Accusing Self

Nafs-i Mulhima: The Inspired Self

Nafs-i Mutmainna: The Peaceful Self

Nafs-i Radhiya: The Pleased Self

Nafs-i Mardhiya: The Pleasing Self

Nafs-i Safiya: The Pure Self

Consider these as levels of consciousness, each more inner and deeper to one's essential reality than the preceding one…

The general notion is that, as a person evolves, he moves out of the station of the Inciting Self and moves on to the station of the Self-Accusing Self, then moves out of the Self-Accusing Self and moves on to the Inspired Self and so on…

But this isn't how it actually works… The person doesn't move anywhere; the understanding and perspective of that particular state becomes disclosed through the person, for all seven stations or states are already present in each person as a whole. They comprise the person. But the person can only observe those that he becomes conscious of.

For example, you can't talk about the Self-Accusing Self to one who is at the station of the Inciting Self. He may look like he understands, but he can't feel it. But one who is at the Self-Accusing Self state will understand the states of the Inciting Self and Inspired Self.

You can't talk about the Peaceful Self to one who is at the station of the Inspired Self, but the one who is at the Peaceful Self state will be aware of the Inspired Self, Self-Accusing and Inciting Self states…

So, these seven levels of the self, though described as though they are different from one another, are actually different states of a single consciousness.

Though it sounds as if one moves from the Inciting Self towards the Pure Self, in terms of how it functions, it actually works the other way around.

Pay attention!

Everything that transpires through you emerges from the state of the Pure Self and becomes manifest through your consciousness. That is, whatever level one may be at, everything that transpires through him, emerges from his Pure Self state and flows towards his current state, from where it becomes manifest.

But because the person is unaware of the states above his current state, he doesn't know where these manifestations come from. Thus, in religious terms, we say, "We came from Allah."

All spiritual stations and levels mentioned in Sufism are fully present in everyone.

Living consciously of them and living unconsciously of them is what makes all the difference.

One who finds these in himself will experience paradise to the extent that he discovers and experiences them. One who fails to discover the higher levels of his essential self will be doomed to the life of multiplicity and thus the experience of hell as a result of it.

Thus, we are advised to view the outside from the inside, to look at matter from the essence, that is, from Oneness to multiplicity, from the world of reality to the world of acts.

When you think of or interact with someone, you can only evaluate them according to the knowledge pertaining to your current level.

This is why they say one at a lower level cannot know the one at a higher level and can only assume them to be like themselves. It's not possible to conceive something beyond your capacity.

Therefore, nobody can change what has been determined for someone else, each will only live what has been determined for themselves, but one may be an apparent cause for another to live what has already been determined for him.

To sum it up, everything you're experiencing originates from the Pure Self state within your own essential depth and becomes manifest through the current level of your consciousness, and sometimes, it becomes manifest without you even being aware. This is what "we come from Allah" means.

The reality that "You can't want unless Allah wants" is also related to this truth.

And so is the verse "It was Allah who threw, not you"…

But because we are generally unaware of the reality hidden in the depths of our consciousness and of how it functions, we judge according to what becomes apparent at our current level of consciousness and thus blame and accuse others and become miserable as a result.

Please realize the importance of this topic and the significance of what I've shared here to lead us out of the delusion we're in.

25.2.99

40

WHO'S TALKING?

"Are you listening to yourself?" or "Do you hear yourself?" we ask sometimes…

But what does it actually mean to listen to one's self? From where do the words we utter originate? The brain you say? But how do they form in the brain? How are they expressed? And why are we bound to live the consequences of the things we say?

Almost everything we live is the direct result of the things we've said or done in the past, most of which we've probably forgotten… Or didn't really take seriously!

We may forget, but Allah doesn't.

We sow what we reap…

Remember the verse:

> **"Whether you conceal what is in your hearts or reveal it, Allah** (as its creator) **knows it."**[19]

You may argue, "But how can I control my thoughts?" Arguing makes no difference my friend.

The system of Allah never falters!

The Rasul (saw) never claimed the mechanics of the system could change if people oppose to them.

Did you ever see an arrow suddenly change its course in the air?

---

[19] Quran 3:29

A thought is like an arrow shot from the brain. As soon as a thought appears in the brain it is already on its way to execution. Allah is the creator of thoughts!

> **"And you threw not** (the arrow) **when you** (illusory self; ego) **threw, but it was Allah who threw!"**[20]

"While it is Allah who created you and all your doings!"

If we conceive the One denoted by the name Allah as a god in space surely, we can't make any sense of this phenomenon, it will seem like a contradiction.

But once we understand the One referenced as Allah is the Ever-living Eternal One in our essence, things will begin to fall into place…

> **"You cannot will unless Allah, the Rabb of the worlds, wills!"**[21]

If we can recognize who's actually behind the seeming act of willing, things will become much more clear…

You're infinitely finite… Allah is infinitely Eternal and Ever-living!

What can nothing create? Nothing!

Everything that appears to exist is the Eternal One!

I only *think* it's *me* who 'wants,' but all of the wanting is emerging only from the Eternal One.

For, "When He wills a thing, He only says to it 'Be' and it is."

Is it the One in space who's willing? Or the *Ghani* and *Baqi* One comprising the essence of all perceivable and unperceivable things?

You make a judgment, your brain executes it, you speak about it and manifest it, and then when you're subject to its consequences you question, "But this isn't what I wanted!?"

My dear friends…

If we want to be of the enlightened ones, let us always be fully conscious of what we speak and recognize who the real speaker is…

---

[20] Quran 8:17

[21] Quran 81:29

If you want to know what He thinks of you, don't ask others, ask yourself, look at your thoughts, what you see in yourself is what He thinks of you!

If you feel you love, then know you are also loved in the sight of Allah.

If you don't feel love but the need to flee, then this is also from Him…

If you're determined to succeed, then He wills you to succeed… If you feel bored and want to move on to something else, then He wills for you to move on to something else…

I don't know if I'm able to express what I'm really trying to say, but if you've understood what I'm pointing to your outlook to many things will change dramatically and your evaluations will bring you much tranquility.

You will begin to see the One who is willing behind the one who is speaking and your suffering will end.

There is no change in the system and there never will be. Everyone will live the consequences of their thoughts and actions.

Thus, it has been said, "Sufficient you are as *Hasib* (holder to account of one's behavioral output)" – a mechanism that won't be in effect sometime in the future, but one that is fully functional at every instance, just like all the other names.

So, let us think good thoughts and remember: whatever we think for others the same will happen to us. Let us never forget this!

The system is fully functional at every instance, ad infinitum!

Allah, is the Ever-living One (*Baqi*)!

25.2.99

Wayne – NJ, USA

41

NOUVEAU RICHE

This pejorative term is generally used in relation to financial wealth. Or shall I say to describe the exaggerated behavior of one who suddenly acquires a significant amount of wealth while lacking a sufficient level of culture and education.

Such people usually do excessive spending to draw attention to themselves aiming to have a superior position over others.

But just like one may be nouveau riche, one may also be *nouveau enlightened*, or a *nouveau Sufi*! That is, acquiring the knowledge pertaining to the level of the Inspired Self (*Nafs-i Mulhima*) without undergoing the necessary spiritual training!

One of the fundamental precepts of Sufism is that the aspirant undergoes intense spiritual training under the guidance of his master (*murshid*). Every master has been trained in a specific way, and so based on these principles, they train the aspirant with whom they've been appointed. This is a comprehensive training entailing mannerisms, habitual behavior, food intake, communication and relationships[22].

Sufi aspirants who undergo the necessary training cease to engage in things like gossiping, taking advantage of others or wanting supremacy, as early as the level of the Self-Accusing Self. This applies to both those who are close to them and those who aren't.

When they reach the level of the Inspired Self, contrary to patronizing others, gossiping and incriminating (as is the case at the level of the Inciting Self) they try to be in service to others to the best of their capacity. For they are fully aware that 'others' are various manifestations of the One, and thus to be in service to them is to be in

[22] Details of how masters act and which techniques they employ can be found in relevant sources.

service to the One, and to rumor and gossip about others is to rumor and gossip about the One!

Sadly, however, true Sufi training ceased many years ago, and most of which seems to be in effect today is merely the name and reputation of a particular Sufi school rather than genuine spiritual training. At least, I haven't seen any!

There are many societies that advocate fear of god and the afterlife, and a craze for paradise, of course! But that's another story… And so, because of this reality, when enthusiastic beginners who lack the necessary groundwork, because they haven't undergone genuine spiritual training, acquire more knowledge than they are capable of carrying, they simply clothe their Inciting Self (*Nafs-i Ammarah*) in the garments of the Inspired Self and become nouveau Sufis!

Just like the truly elite and noble socialites eventually recede from gatherings the nouveau riche begin to populate, genuine Sufis withdraw from societies in which nouveau Sufis seem to be in prominence. They simply retreat and observe in silence…

Those who complain about not getting results even though they have apparently spent so much time and done such and such practice, first need to overcome their Inciting Self!

It's easy to say "I am" and slay the rest of creation; it's easy to claim enlightenment and rebuke everyone else!

One who has really reached the level of the Inspired Self will do justice to everything and everyone he encounters, seeing them as a trust from Allah.

If a man, he will do justice to his wife and effectively give her due. If a woman, she will do justice to her husband, family and femininity. Claiming to be in service to Allah without accomplishing these is nothing other than consecrating a delusional god!

Inability to see the One in the face of your spouse or children, and approaching them in respect of their apparent veil, reveals nothing other than your own veil.

Just because one who centers his life on food and sex talks eloquently about the Pure Self and the Pleasing Self doesn't mean he has overcome his Inciting Self!

Many are at the level of the Inciting Self, but are dressed as the Inspired Self. Their knowledge of the Inspired Self has become their antichrist, leading them to choose the paradise of the antichrist!

The antichrist may become disclosed in one's mind, or in one's environment, or in a nation against a society, or against the entire world! Just like death is experienced at the individual level as it is at the societal level, the same applies to the antichrist. It is an archetype and may take different forms at different levels. Its function is to cause confusion between what is right and what is wrong, what is authentic and what is unauthentic, what is proper and what is improper, etc. – showing the right in the guise of the wrong and vice versa… In other words, its function is to twist, distort and misguide.

In terms of the individual, the antichrist archetype becomes most explicit at the level of the Inspired Self. If the person hasn't received the necessary spiritual training, his misgivings will provide extra support, leading his ego to become pharaonic and thus eternally veiled.

The people of authenticity will READ the system and articulate things that have not been previously spoken of while the people of inauthenticity will spend much of their time in idle talk and hearsay.

In the end, everyone will find what they deserve!

5.5.99

Note: This is not an attack on anyone. The source of this article is none other than the reflection in my mirror.

42

EMOTION VS INTELLECT

How do the defense and projection mechanisms of our mind work? How do our reactions form?

Why do our children or spouse fervently defend themselves immediately after we try to correct their mistakes?

I'm neither a psychologist nor a psychiatrist, but I have an opinion…

The brain is a whole, but in terms of its intellectual activity we can divide it into two:

Intellectual activity that we're aware of, and activity that we're not aware of.

Thoughts and ideas arising from our **higher consciousness** involve our awareness, logic and intellect.

Thoughts and ideas that we're not aware of are produced by the database in our **subconscious**.

The thoughts and emotions produced in our subconscious are derived from a few sources, including the genetic code we inherit, incoming waves from our environment as of birth, the conditioning that we are prone to throughout our lives, and the information we receive from what we read, watch and who we make contact with. All of this forms the database comprising our subconscious mind.

Our higher consciousness, on the other hand, has the ability to evaluate things within a systematic framework based on the criteria of universal truths.

Reasoning is the ability to probe and examine the things that we're aware of through conscious evaluation. Used in a systematic framework, it's called 'logic.' If there is no systematic thought, then we say it's illogical.

Most of our lives are governed by our subconscious minds. The difference between the instinctual behavior of other animals and us is their lack of intellectual potential.

No matter which country or which society they're from, all people have a subconscious and almost everyone is governed by it. Hence, the subconscious has also been called the person's devil. The mind is the source of intellectual activity produced by the subconscious.

The mechanism that controls this is the higher consciousness: wisdom and intellect.

One can spend his entire life relying on his mind. Logic can be used both by the mind and the intellect. If one is a person of wisdom and intellect, he'll have the capacity to contemplate on life after death and become receptive to universal truths. He'll live his life based on the truths of the hereafter and act accordingly.

A clever person relying on his mind, on the other hand, will use his logic and think about all the ways he can best live his worldly life, and if it befits his scenario, he may reach great success.

The question I was asked was:

"Why is it that when I say something in an attempt to correct my child or my spouse they immediately begin to defend themselves and not only am I not heard but I'm also attacked?"

First of all, the person doesn't begin to defend himself consciously. That is, he doesn't show this response after listening to you, hearing you out, and then using his reason and logic to evaluate what you're saying. This response is the direct reflection of his clever defense mechanism in his subconscious mind!

One begins to form solid ideas about certain things as of childhood. These ideas become fixed with age, and when you say something that goes against these ideas, he automatically defends himself, without any conscious thought. This is his way of asserting his identity. Most times, he doesn't even have time to use his logic and wit! Thus, he begins to say illogical things and even begin to insult in order to defend his identity.

As for why the subconscious mind is the person's devil:

The fixed and conditioned data in the brain's database forms either through genetic inheritance or from one's environment. They are generally adopted and taken as fact without verification or authentication.

Now, when the person encounters a truth that opposes his database, he initially reacts and denies it. This is because the mind works in a way to defend and protect existing data. The mind always works in favor of the existing database, not the universal truths based on the system!

As a result, incoming new information is generally denied and rejected without intellectual logical evaluation.

So, when one encounters an idea that goes against his lifestyle or the society in which he lives, he will choose to defend his existing database and reject the new idea at the expense of gaining hew insight and spiritual advancement. Because of this deprivation, the mind has been referred to as the person's devil.

If the subconscious cannot be controlled via the intellect, then the person will be controlled and governed by the database comprising his subconscious mind.

This is why the Rasuls and Nabis were always rejected! For they warned the people in line with the universal realities and advised them to shape their lives according to these truths.

Those who oppose this, whether it be the daughter of a friend or the daughter of a Rasul, are simply reflecting the defense mechanism of their subconscious mind.

The expression, "I turned my devil into a Muslim" means, "I have my subconscious under control and in line with the universal truths."

All forms of suffering and remorse result from the actions driven by the subconscious.

Faith cannot be an imitation, but some of the practices that have been advised as the requisites of Islam can be imitated.

One without wisdom and intellect cannot have faith!

Faith is the result of the higher consciousness evaluating the universal realities within a logical framework and acknowledging the creator of this universal system and order.

The Rasul is one who recognizes the universal truths within his essence and higher consciousness and warns others based on the reality disclosed from his essence.

Those who conceive a god in space imagine the angels to be like objects or entities sent to earth from space. Those who recognize Allah as the creator of the only universal reality are aware of the indivisibility of His Power and that the angel called Spirit comprises the essence of all created things. They know, therefore, that Gabriel does not come from space and the force called "*Azrail*" is an angelic mechanism within every created form.

Ideas produced by the subconscious are given an imaginary form in the brain and evaluated by the higher consciousness. Therefore, man is constantly living in his imagination (i.e. holographic world).

While some squander their lives under the control of their subconscious, or rely on their intelligence to 'speak' fancily of faith… Others use their higher consciousness to evaluate and experience faith, shaping and changing their lives according to these truths.

There is no room for excuse in the system!

There is no compensation in the system!

The system does not allow giving intellect to one who lacks it!

Many live in the guise of a human in this system, but not all of them pass on as one.

24.6.99

43

STABILITY

It's difficult to find stability!

It's difficult to be stable.

It's hard to think and live in a stable way…

Only a select few have accomplished this!

To wake up in stability.

To remain stable while awake.

To be stable while working.

To be stable with your spouse.

To be in stability while eating.

To live the worldly life in stability.

To live in your own world in stability.

To be in stable relationships with your world and the system…

You exist within a system and order, and you always will.

Either you comply with the requisites of this system, live in balance and stability and transform your world into paradise, observing the manifestations of Allah at every instance…

Or, you turn down the blessings that are being showered upon you and hold on to the itsy bits of information you've gathered from here and there, showing it off like the nouveau riche, totally off-balance!

A day will come when all that you know will be erased… You'll find yourself repeating the few lines you've memorized "I AM the One!" "You are the One!" "Everything is One" blah blah blah…

To establish balance in one's life and to be able to assimilate or handle things in life are two of the most important matters...

To be able to handle human relations...

To be able to handle and assimilate knowledge...

To be able to handle the world, and *your* world!

One who can handle and assimilate things is one with balance and stability – in every field – one who does not feel the need to show off, or to gain acceptance from others, or to prove himself to anyone...

Unity is experienced in the heavens!

The world is the plane of multiplicity, where the requisites of the system and order are disclosed...

The heavens are forever eternal!

Your world is forever eternal!

Be careful! Don't take the heavens and world as space and earth like the ignorant ones!

The unstable ones try to pull heaven down to the earth... Yes, the earth is in space, but it is governed by its own set of laws... Computing brains don't get this!

When one does not cleanse himself of his emotions it automatically results in being unbalanced and unstable, for emotions blind the eye of the intellect...

The user of knowledge, at all levels, is always the intellect. Whether it be Transcendental Intelligence (*Aql al-Ma'ad*) or the Universal Intellect (*Aql al-Qull*) or the First Intellect (*Aql al-Awwal*) it does not matter, it is always the Intellect that appraises knowledge.

The Intellect is the manifestation of the attribute of knowledge on the face of creation.

Knowledge is higher than gnosis, for knowledge is an attribute that condescends, while gnosis is disclosed from the servant and aids in ascension.

This is why there is no attribute such as 'gnosis' among the attributes of Allah, but there is an attribute called 'knowledge' referenced by the name '*al-Alim.*'

Knowledge isn't the information given in the faculty of science or the Sufi classes taught in the faculty of Arts!

As Yunus Emre asserts, "Knowledge is to comprehend knowledge; knowledge is to know yourself!" That is, knowledge is the divine Self-disclosure of the creator of the heavens and the earth!

One who knows himself will be able to assimilate…

One who knows himself will have balance and stability…

One who knows himself will do justice by the system and order…

One who knows himself will be true to himself and do justice by his servitude!

One who fails to accomplish these is not a person of knowledge but a person of memorization, not very different to a computer's hard drive!

But what if one asks, "Stable or unstable according to *who*?"

Remember one with stability is unstable in the perception of an unstable one!

Hence, we may say, if one has a clear conscience, a peaceful and tranquil life, is able to observe the beauty of Allah at all times, has been moralized with the morals of Allah, can assimilate knowledge and live accordingly, then this person has balance and stability! This person lives not for himself but to be of benefit to others, even if this may require seclusion and retreat!

But one who causes provocation and stirs trouble among people, gossips, rumors, and shows ingratitude, is clearly an unstable person.

To expect reverence and respect from others, to not suffice with spirituality and pursue the wealth of the world, to claim superiority and authority over others are all signs of not being able to handle and assimilate certain blessings…

May Allah bless us with true friends, those with stability and assimilation, and always keep us on the path of knowledge and stability!

3.4.99

NJ – USA

44

THE REALITY

The judgment belongs to Allah!

The sovereignty belongs to Allah!

He who does not judge with the judgment of Allah is a denier of the reality!

> **"Those who do not judge by what Allah revealed, they are deniers of the reality!"[23]**

> **"And whoever does not judge in accordance with what Allah reveals, they are the wrongdoers."[24]**

> **"Whoever does not judge with the creeds revealed by Allah, they are the corrupters!"[25]**

They are **deniers of the reality** because, by denying the truth, they are covering the source of what has been revealed.

They are **wrongdoers** because, by not doing justice to the reality, they are doing wrong to themselves.

They are **corrupters** because, by failing to recognize their essential reality, they are living with a corrupted concept of 'self'.

Let's dive a little deeper now:

If we look with a conditioned understanding of "god" as a powerful being in space who judges with the laws he sends down to his selected servants on earth…

---

[23] Quran 5:44
[24] Quran 5:45
[25] Quran 5:47

But if we understand what is referenced by the name "Allah" and possess the capacity to contemplate on its implications, we can see that:

There is a Single Absolute Universal Judge present in every iota of existence, and it is only this judgment that is in effect in the universe at all times!

Thus, the **denier** covers the reality because he lacks the insight and foresight to see this Absolute Judge…

The **wrongdoer** does wrong to himself because he assumes himself to be *other than* or *outside* the Absolute Judge, hence falling into duality and becoming veiled from his essential Self…

And the **corrupter** fails to observe the Absolute Judge in his essence; his conditioning and value judgments corrupt his consciousness, making him see and evaluate everything in a distorted way…

Now in this light, let us touch on a topic I discussed in the *Mystery of Man…*

According to the religion of Islam and Sufism, when one puts forth harmful or offensive behavior, we are advised to be *amicable to the offender but condemn the offence…* What this means is, we are advised to condemn and estrange from the offensive action, yet in light of the understanding "To love the created for the sake of the creator" to not reduce our love for the person!

The Absolute Judge does everything for a particular reason and purpose, which defines the wisdom behind the creation of that thing. Whether in our view it is good or bad, it does not change anything.

Fatwa is not one of the fundamental principles of religion! Fatwa can never be an excuse to save you from the consequence of your actions. Fatwa is merely an opinion.

If a fatwa is based on a rigid-minded restricted view and goes against the reality, it will lead all its followers astray!

So, we must realize the truth that:

Everything that transpired HAD TO transpire, it couldn't have *not* happened! It was definitely and absolutely going to happen – regardless – and so it did! As for everything that didn't happen, it couldn't have happened anyway, it was only an assumption and so it did not happen!

To each individual their own creational purpose and life path, and everything that will lead to it, has been eased…

So, what kind of attitude should we have toward one who is veiled from his reality and who lives a body-centered life?

To advise the truth… It is our duty!

But if one rejects this advice, then *to not persist* is also our duty!

If that person's outlook and behavior isn't in line with ours, then we can simply say "May Allah give guidance and peace" and continue on our way…

Our paths cross with many people during our life… With some we walk together and with others, due to the difference of our creational make-up, our paths part soon after meeting… Everyone travels in the path that is in line with their creational make-up and purpose…

And yes, a day may come and you may become teary, remembering all the people that were once dear and near but who have all left your life, one by one…

Separations are inevitable my friend… They are bound to happen until our last breath… But perhaps a few friends will remain close to you, enough of them to carry you to your grave…

Ah tolerance… Tolerance…

To see the Judge behind the judgment!

To see Allah behind the Judge!

To see that even the Rasuls fulfill only their servitude…

My friend…

Urgently adopt the morals of Allah and befriend the friends of Allah so the traitors around you do not cause your demise!

You may be so veiled as to throw your loved ones into the fire and then claim "This was the divine decree!"…

But the reality is:

Your end is determined by your means. That is, what you are the means for is what will determine your end.

If after knowledge has come to you, you choose to follow your transitory hankerings, you will be of those who wrong themselves.

Say, "My Rabb is Allah!" and adopt the morals of Allah so that you may judge with His Judgment.

Otherwise, you're bound to be either a denier of reality, a wrongdoer or a corrupter.

May Allah allow us to be of those who fulfill their servitude with a lifestyle befitting vicegerents.

10.6.99

45

TRUST IN ALLAH (*TAWAKKUL*)

The limited in understanding recklessly claim, "I have placed my trust in Allah" without taking any precautions. Clearly, they don't know that the act of '*tawakkul*,' without first taking the necessary precautions, is generally what the foolish do!

The Rasul of Allah (saw) says: "Tie your camel first, and then trust in Allah."

It is well known how Caliphate Hadhrat Omar (ra) went to Damascus with his army and told his army to turn back after hearing there was plague in the city. When they asked him, "Are you fleeing from the fate of Allah?" he answered, "I am retreating to Allah's judgment from Allah's fate!"

I have been writing about the absolute and unchangeable nature of fate since 1965, so have I changed my mind… You may be wondering?

Absolutely not!

Whatever my understanding of fate was in 1965 that is the understanding I have today and I have discussed it in full detail in my previous books. Nevertheless, I see that the 'precaution-trust' dilemma still isn't fully grasped by the majority.

I know and believe with absolute certainty that fate is absolute and not subject to change!

Even the precautions we take are the *result* of our fate, not contrary to or outside of it!

Whatever the conditions we are subject to, if there's room to take precautions, whether small or significant, strong or feeble, vast or little, we must take them immediately! Conscious of the fact that even the precautions we take are determined by our fate!

The mistake is often made in thinking precautions can change the determination!

I had written "Precautions are also from predestination" in *The Great Awakening*[26] 35 years ago!

The world is the abode of wisdom, and everything that occurs is formed by the events that have led up to it. This is the universal system and order of Allah.

If one claims to have placed their trust in Allah without having taken any precautions, then quite obviously taking precautions has not been predetermined for them. This is also from fate.

True entrustment is to see that everything is formed with the determination of Allah.

To assign Allah as your essential agent (*wakil*) is to activate your internal precaution mechanism – not to resort to an external god. Please try to understand this well.

The masses take precautions, but do not place their trust in Allah.

The noble don't take precautions, they say "It is what it is" and fully place their trust in Allah.

The elite take the necessary precautions, fully conscious and in observation of the One making the determination…

This is where concealed duality is totally removed and the observer becomes Itself!

April 17, 1999, is the first day of the Islamic lunar year. The new moon is in Aries, making this year an important beginning…

The world is also moving into the Age of Aquarius. Chiron will move into Scorpio in June and give the Scorpions and the rising Scorpions a last chance to find guidance until October, before moving into Sagittarius. Here, Chiron will conjunct with Pluto and make a sextile angle with Uranus and Neptune, as it awaits the 'White Horse'…

The chain of events that transpire reflect the will of Allah, and as they do, we shall observe, as best we can… Though the foolish don't

[26] Chapter 18

know that denying these cosmic effects is like denying the energy we receive from the honey we eat…

The gnostic talks about trust in Allah, putting precaution aside…

The scholar and the successor apply every form of precaution they possibly can, knowing precautions are also from the predetermination of Allah…

Everything was predetermined to transpire exactly as it does, before the creation of the universe, to transpire as a single instance of creation, filtered through the creation's concept of 'time'… All as 'nothing' in the sight of the creator…

Some are going to fight and war, as per the scenario, and some are going to laugh and rejoice! And then the curtain is going to close, once again…

All strength (motion, action, transformation and state of tasbih) and power (with which this is carried out) is with Allah!

HU!

17.4.99

46

FROM HERE AND THERE

Words once spoken are like milk suckled from a mother's breast – it can't be put back!

A thought, once it arises, is like an arrow from a bow – it can't be stopped… Until it makes its owner live the consequences.

The heart also has an owner!

An excuse is nothing but self-deception, it has no place in the system, other than empty solace.

When that day comes (is it in the future?) no one will be asked to give an excuse.

A wound on a knee will heal, but the wound caused by the tongue… Very difficult!

The system is all about the things we do and their consequences. There is no compensation for betrayal!

The path to hell is filled with good intentions, my friend!

Intelligence will help you save the day, but it will also produce food for the 'others'!

Whoever you're with in your world now is whom you'll be with in the next…

If your external is a veil to your internal and your essence then you will pass on to the next world in a state veiled from Allah.

The angels that hold to account are made of pure NUR, thcy have no form, but every person perceives them differently in the grave. Why?

Every mind has a different way of decoding things; when reason and intellect is put aside, the fruits of the crafty and cunning mind come into play, but be careful! These fruits may be poisonous!

Tyranny may enslave the intellect and logic, but only temporarily, not indefinitely.

Success resulting from treachery can never be lasting.

Death, for one who has nothing left to lose, is nothing other than a reward.

The want to dominate and rule over others is the reflection of the Inciting Self.

The people of spirituality have no business with politics; only those who are expelled from spirituality engage in such things.

The jungle is where brute force rules; the physically strong have the upper hand and the weak are overturned.

The place where force and compulsion isn't used, where people don't tyrannize each other is called the city.

One who is different on the inside and different on the outside will also have a different afterlife to their worldly life.

All things will change one day... Even kings and kingdoms lose their authority and power!

I exist not for the people but for Allah!

Your world is your business not mine.

You can't know yourself until you forego your 'self'! When you know yourself you will know 'me.'

The label in your head will never stick on me. Nobody found me where they went.

What you can't find in *your* world you can never find in *the* world.

Everything is inverted in the world of the antichrist.

So long as the Mahdi doesn't emerge from your essence you can't find guidance in your world.

The door to repentance is open until the last breath, but you can never compensate for the past.

My friend, stop trying to find a beloved like yourself and make Allah your beloved.

47

DARK CLOUDS

The creator has created! A system is in progress. A mechanism; a living organism: the Universe! We are all in it.

There is no room for emotion in this organism. Only functions and consequences are of concern. And interactions and chained reactions like ripple effects, where every formation is an extension of another formation…

Societies are like the human body. The human body is a miniature universe.

Just like when too much bacteria accumulates in the body sickness emerges. When too much bacteria accumulates in a society, the society becomes ill. Bacteria don't act out of emotions, they have no mercy, they only execute their function. 'God' believers call their god in space to account. And when they can't understand the message, they try to find solace in Muhammad (saw) in their dreams and attempt to comfort themselves by "damning bacteria!"

Those who inject into their bodies the very germs they want to get rid of are no different to those who bombard the masses with missiles in the name of peace-making…

While hundreds of thousands of people, recently in Bosnia and today in Kosovo, were under the threat of extinction, they were consoling themselves with Sufi tales, claiming "This is the manifestation of the One, too" while eating and drinking and entertaining themselves as though they will not face the consequences of their heedless acts.

Dark, black clouds are gathering in the sky…

No account can be settled unless the bill is paid.

Those who watched the catastrophe in Bosnia will also have their turn. That account has not been settled, the bills have not been paid…

There are bills to be paid and accounts to be settled!

The mechanism is at work. The cogwheels of the mechanism have no mercy. They only know to engage with one another, smashing up whatever comes between them.

When the dark clouds release their rain, all those who stand under it will get wet. The rain doesn't consider whether it's falling upon the good or the bad. It just rains and wets.

Dangerous black smoke is being created by those whose functions are 'bad.' The sky above Europe is getting dark.

Taking advantage of this darkness in Europe, there is a group of people waiting to spread darkness to other places too. But no need to worry, clouds come and go, they are not everlasting.

Dark clouds destroy their creators first and then themselves!

And the sun will rise again, over the good. And the ill will get better…

Times will change, darkness will give way to light, the afflicted will recover, and all suffering will come to an end, giving everyone what they deserve.

There are also those who worry in respect of their human nature, but who are actually in undisturbed observation and stillness in terms of their essential reality. They quietly observe the sickness, the causers of the sickness and the ones exhausted and abolished by the sickness absolve away…

Thus is man! What has he got to give away? Some have their life. Some have an enormous world filled with possessions…

It's said that some spirits will leave the body with great pain and difficulty, and some will abandon the body effortlessly and smoothly.

As Bill Donahue says in Zen, if you die before you're dead, you don't die when you're dead.

But if you live just for profligacy and are constantly looking for ways to take advantage of people, then you are functioning as a germ. That means your way leads you to fire and burning is inevitable. As it turns out, fire is sometimes the best sterilizer.

A surgeon does not hesitate to cut off a gangrenous organ. He doesn't approach the patient with meaningless pity; as he aims to save the patient, and thus he does whatever is necessary. In the same light, when one begins to cut off the gangrenous areas in his life, among all the areas invaded by germs, inevitably some uncontaminated areas are gone too. A big fish is bigger than a small fish, but there is always a bigger fish than a big fish… There are things we can see of the unseen and things we can't see of the seen, thus is the case up to the Throne.

Though, of course, there will always be those who consider the Throne as a literal, gigantic, celestial royal chair, like little children who don't understand metaphors and search for the truth within the symbol. Apparently, they find Allah "within" themselves and so they claim to find him within others as well… Whatever "within" means…

Where is Allah within? Within what? Within who? Within me, within you, within a man, within a woman, within the germ??!! Within those who don't get the difference between taking lessons from past and bearing a grudge??!!

Is Allah within an atom? In a body cell? Inside the body? In the brain? Or in the spirit?

I hear you saying "Allah is free and beyond the manifest corporeal worlds (*al-Ghani*)!"

They call me Ahmed Hulusi, but who am "I"? Am I a world or a particle? What am I? Who and what exactly are they referencing with this name?

But anyway, what's it to us, let's go out and have some fun, eat, drink, listen to so-and-so then go to bed. Why bother ourselves with so many questions and all the problems they bring along.

Contemplating such matters has not been made easy for us. Every bird flies with its flock they say. Whatever we've been created for is what seems easy for us.

Turn into yourself and find out what has been made easy for you, that you may understand the purpose of your creation and find your own flock.

Time is ticking and dark clouds are gathering in the sky… "So, flee to Allah," my friends… Flee to Allah…

48

AWAKENING

Though we awaken from a different dream every morning, what makes us think we're not going to suddenly awaken one day from the dream of this world?

When we wake up and find nobody to argue and quarrel with, what kind of a situation are we going to be in, I wonder?

Are we aware that we are a test for each other?

We're in a test with the mentally ill, the schizophrenic, the dictators, the senile, those with personality problems, or those with an inferiority complex, or a superiority complex…

They're going to live the consequences of their life when they wake up, but what about those who got engrossed and caught up by them?

Such people usually cause provocation to their environment. Often even their closest won't know what they are doing. They introduce themselves differently, but then engage in certain behaviors that nobody really knows, thus they can cause provocation to their closest too.

The only way to be protected from provocation (*fitnah*) is with knowledge.

Fitnah won't end until you render it ineffective. Your only choice is to become immune to it, in this world, or in the grave, or in hell!

If you don't want to wake up in regret, don't get caught up in fitnah, my friend.

If you want to get to know people, step on their toes, but be ready to face the consequences, for then their true self will emerge.

The level of one's maturity will be revealed when their material or non-material benefits are harmed.

If someone is trying too hard to get acceptance and acknowledgement then clearly, he has no trust in himself or his knowledge, he has a personality problem.

If someone accuses me of something and I try to convince them otherwise I would be taking the accusations seriously and trying to prove myself. The most appropriate approach to take in a situation like this would be to say "May Allah give you peace. You're free to think and believe what you like" and move on…

The people and events that transpire around us are like test questions. Regardless of who and what comprises your environment, if you take knowledge as your guide you will not go astray.

Don't take anyone as an example. Don't forget, nobody is perfect.

Befriend for knowledge not for gossip!

If one gossips he is devoid of knowledge, this is a fact! No matter how much knowledge one may seem to have, if he engages in gossip, then he has not gone past the Inciting Self.

Hold firmly to knowledge and follow its path.

Being near or close to an enlightened being will not serve you unless you change the course of your life and stop engaging in inferior behavior. Try to see the knowledge, not the body or the person! Those who turn to other 'bodies' are eventually going to separate from them, but one who turns to knowledge will never be deprived.

Those who take others as examples will eventually encounter actions or behaviors that go against their belief and fall into confusion. But one who turns to the knowledge disclosed by the Rasul (saw) will never feel regret and will definitely reach his purpose.

It is totally possible to be awakened in this world!

If in the face of an adversity you can say, "The *Malik'ul Mulk* – the One who governs His Sovereignty as He wishes – has subjected me to this situation" and not waste any time and effort on the seeming offenders you will have turned to your essential reality. The best thing to do in the face of any adverse situation is to turn inward, to their true Owner… Remember the verse "flee to Allah" denotes an introspective action!

There are many alleged saints who deify their ego after the station of the Inspired Self and fall right back into the Inciting Self state and die in denial!

A saint will never put forth actions that go against the teachings of the Quran.

A saint will never engage in gossip or be ungrateful.

A saint will never patronize others or expect others to serve him.

A saint will not expose the faults and mistakes of others. He is forgiving.

A saint never tries to prove a point or takes part in verbal debates.

A saint knows that everyone is with whom they deserve to be.

A saint knows the value of knowledge and doesn't reduce its esteem by running after people who don't cherish it.

A saint is peaceful and content; he is protected from the provocations of the Inspired Self and the evil commands of the Inciting Self.

Those who choose to follow their fancy desires after knowledge has come to them, who use the knowledge pertaining to the station of the Inspired Self to rule over others with their Inciting Self are bound to suffer.

May Allah protect us all from such people!

26.4.99

49

TEST

And how about when we're told that we're being "tested"...

We start to think... Who is testing us? Why is he testing us? Does he not already know if we'll pass or not? Who are we to oppose his judgment anyway? And what will happen if we can't pass the test? How long are we going to be tested for?

It's funny how we automatically think that we're being tested by someone 'out there'... As if he set up the world as a test arena and sent us all here for his amusement, happily observing how we're all struggling...

It's funny how we think the sun rises and sets for us... And the seasons change for us, and that plants and animals are all to serve us, and that all the galaxies and in fact the universe exists for us!

The average human life span is equivalent to about eight seconds in terms of a solar year... In this light; I would suggest man stops taking himself so seriously and wakes up to the reality...

Nobody out there is testing you!

The creator has created the system and told us "Know yourself, find Me in yourself, adopt my morals and live accordingly."

The sun isn't rising and setting for you, the rain isn't falling for you! You found yourself in the midst of events... And you can either be in the best of conduct, in line with the teachings of the Rasul (saw) and thus your essential reality... Or, put your knowledge and intellect aside, and act according to your primitive conditioning and judgments, ending up in a regretful state that can't be compensated!

Every situation you encounter at every moment is a test... It is the test of your knowledge!

If you make the right response you will be lead to new questions and situations…

If you make the wrong response you will be lead to other questions and situations…

Whatever you do, you can't go back to a question you've already answered.

The system is ruthless.

It is definite.

And immutable.

The system hasn't been created for you. You just found yourself in this system.

"I created the worlds for you" was addressed to the Reality of Muhammad (saw) – the POINT!

Our bodies are no more than food for the worms and birds. The earth has a way of putting us in our place if we don't act fast and learn our place before it's too late.

Man is one who is smart enough to think about his happiness not just in his immediate future, but also in his future after death.

I've spent 54 years in vain… I've earned nothing. I'm in absolute need, externally and internally… I still haven't figured the workings of the system in which I exist. I'm still expecting miracles! I'm expecting the sun to rise from the west for me, and for the Satan and the Antichrist to abandon their ways for me…

The system is calling out to me at every instant, but my ears have become deaf, my eyes blind, and my heart seems to have become sealed; I am unable to perceive the truths of the system…

We reap what we sow my friends…

Being HUman is so much more than the label we think it to be…

10.5.99

50

PARADISE – HEAVEN

Who wants to end up in paradise? Who doesn't?

Some say they prefer hell because it's filled with models and dancers and pop stars(!) And some, more selfless, claim "I don't want heaven, I want YOU," though nobody really knows who or what they're actually referring to by 'YOU'…

So, what is the life of paradise like then? Who will be there? How will they get there? Where is it? etc. etc. So many questions… But beware, if you dig too much, they'll either call you an unbeliever or a denier! Don't use your brain, don't think, don't question, don't even wonder…! You've been forbidden to question!

But what can I say, my curiosity got the better of me… So, I did my research… And after synthesizing the results with modern scientific findings, I deduced an understanding. Needless to say, this is my personal construal; you are free not to take it seriously if it doesn't make sense to you.

Now, just as paradise means something in terms of worldly life, it also means something in terms of the life of the grave. Of course, there is also a paradise in the absolute sense. So, when someone uses the word paradise in reference to only one of these meanings it leads to misunderstanding.

When we say paradise in the worldly sense we generally think of an environment or state of supreme pleasure. Paradise in terms of the grave, however, is quite different… After all, matter-based perception ends in the grave and the person transits to the life of the grave. If their destination is paradise, they will begin to live in a state referred to as the paradise of the grave.

The person begins to perceive heaven and hell after they are fully in the realm of the grave, with a spiritual perception. The five senses no longer exist here. Instead, the person uses his spirit perception, as much as he was able to develop it during the worldly life, to convert incoming waves of information. Let's call this the spirit-brain for now… In the realm of the grave, the person perceives the life of hell and the life of heaven, alongside other spiritual beings and angels, feeling fear and longing at the same time.

Just like in our dreams, our emotions and thoughts are symbolized by certain images. Similarly, in the life of the grave, the person observes and experiences the automatic results of his life in the world, either as pleasure or as nightmare…

At this point, all connection to earthly life has ceased. The person can now only perceive certain energies and prayers that are directed to him or certain Quranic messages, as much as he can understand… But none of this engages him for too long. It's like a one way receiver. The waves that are formed in the spirit brain are at such high frequencies compared to our current brains that it is impossible for us to perceive and decode them. The human brain can at most perceive frequencies from the jinn, and even that is subject to certain conditions and terms.

Emotions that are felt during the dream state are experienced at much higher intensities in the life of the grave.

This is true until Doomsday, or until the sun engulfs the earth. When the sun begins to engulf the earth, all human spirits will find themselves in a state of hell, the dimension of the sun-waves… This is generally stated as 'people arising from their graves' in religious literature.

The energy (Nur) one has accumulated by applying the recommended practices (prayers, mantras, etc.) during his worldly life will allow him to escape from this state of hell to heaven, depending on the strength and level of Nur they've acquired…

What I mean by escaping from hell is they will leave their spirit body in hell and move on to another new dimension with their Nur bodies.

Just like we leave our physical bodies in the world and move on to the grave with our spirit bodies, we will also leave our spirit bodies, if we are to go to heaven, and wear our Nur bodies.

Essentially, every form and creation has a spirit and Nur state. Even the sun has a spirit and a Nur state. Because we only perceive the physical state of the sun, we can't see the beings pertaining to the spirit and Nur state of the sun.

Those who can see with the eye of the spirit can perceive the Nur dimension, though this dimension has no particular structure as it is pure consciousness, and consciousness experiences what it wills instantaneously here, as though it is physical, like in a dream.

The power of the person in heaven is equivalent to how much he can use his ability to actualize his dreams and his potentials. This is true for the world too.

The shape and form of the body in the spirit realm is usually based on the state just before the person dies.

Nur beings are free of form and shape; they can take the shape of whatever they like.

All Nur beings in heaven are conscious beings, and the form they take depends on the database of the person by whom they wish to be perceived.

This is also why the angels of account in the grave appear differently to everyone.

The names of Allah will manifest in heaven, to the extent of the person's knowledge, and the person will be able to use the strength and power of Allah to create whatever they want whenever they want.

19.4.99

51

WHAT'S YOUR EXTENSION?

Just like you can't change the format of a file by changing the extension in its name, you can't become a Sufi or a Muslim by calling yourself one.

Which god are you kidding by performing salat as if you're doing gymnastics, having no clue as to what you're reciting? Which reality are you witnessing by repeating the Word of Unity and the Word of Testimony without ever once considering the reality it points to? When are you going to understand the difference between the name and the *named*, and that the named does not change when you change its name?

It's common sense to know that claiming to be this or that isn't sufficient to get you to heaven. If all you do is try "fixing" other people and forcing them to be "Muslims," instead of strengthening your own inner faith, then you are far from the reality of Islam even if you call yourself a Muslim. Remember Muhammad (saw) had said "At the end of times, a thousand Muslims will fill a mosque, but there won't be single person with genuine faith among them."

Today, 1.5 billion people comprise the Muslim population, let's assume this is more than the Christian population; if you think this is victory, you're wrong; it's merely self-deception. If one is dedicated to names and labels, he can't READ the Quran; he can only pronounce its letters. Remember, names and words function as indicators; they only serve to help you to find your way. Instead of collecting and carrying them along with you, try following them, try finding the reality they reference. When you read something, try to see the message it's trying to convey, rather than merely pronouncing its letters.

They say the word '*riba*' for example means 'interest' and is 'forbidden,' without really considering the type of application it actually references. In a country with a 100% inflation rate, they set their eyes on a retired employee's piggy bank savings and intimidate him with hellfire. Yet, when they change the word 'interest' to 'profit share' in an alleged Islamic bank system, it suddenly becomes legit!

'Don't look at illegitimate things!' they say and they cover their heads and eyes and refuse to watch TV, oblivious of the fact that 'to not look' actually means 'to not *desire* the illegitimate'!

So consumed with names and labels, they fall far from the true meaning of the message.

He says 'Allah,' they make it 'God.'

He says 'Rasul,' they make it 'prophet.'

He says 'the Heavens,' they make it 'sky/space.'

He says 'understand the system of Allah through Islam,' but they choose to be content with being 'Muslim.'

They fall far from Muhammad's (saw) path of faith, but they are so sure they're on the right path.

1.5.1999

52

SELL YOURSELF TO ALLAH

Animals, as known, make their living using brute-force. They prey and attack. If they have the power to capture their prey they do everything in their power to capture, and thus they maintain their living. The tears of their prey don't mean anything for them. They have no pity. All they care about is capturing an animal that is weaker than them, whether openly or by way of a trap. They don't care if their prey has a partner, children, family, etc. They don't have such emotions. They are animals.

As for humans, they make their living in various ways... Some sell, some lease, some are sold and some are leased, some sell their property, some sell their body, and some their faith and soul...

Some are bought by Allah, and some by His servants... Don't you remember the verse, "Indeed, Allah has purchased from the believers, their souls and their properties..."

Some fulfill their servitude through faith, some fulfill their servitude through denial, but only those who've reached the state of unveiling can observe this.

Some are bought out by other creatures; they're financed over longer periods. Once their price has been fully paid, they are completely owned.

Many make their living via rental income. Some lease out their house, some their car, and some their money. But the more serious cases involve those who rent out their brains, their speech, their organs and souls.

Life is hard my friends... It's hard to live without becoming a servant to someone, without running into trouble...

Yet Allah is both the investor and the customer. Why some don't choose Him as a customer I do not understand…

How you spend your rental income is important. To whom you're sold or leased out is also very important. It directly affects your eternal life.

Life is all about business.

You can never own something if you don't pay its worth.

So, if you want to know the price Allah is willing to give you, READ the book.

Time is ticking; the only organ that does not devaluate with time is a brain full of knowledge, gnosis and faith.

So, if you're going to sell yourself, sell your self to Allah.

If you're going to lease yourself out, let Allah lease you.

And never look down upon anyone!

16.6.99

53

FOR "GOD'S" SAKE!

When I was around 15 years old, I was an atheist. The idea of a god in space seemed too primitive a notion for me, especially the idea of the delivery-men-prophets he sent to earth. The only reality I could accept was that there had to be a creator of the universe that I perceived. During that time, I was giving English lessons to high school students and also doing voice-over recordings.

On September 10, 1963, when I was 17, my father left this world…

The Friday that came three days after, my mother, who was born in Mecca and blessed on the doorsill of the *Kaaba* – as was the custom – pleaded that I attend the congregational Friday prayer and that I pray for my late father…

So, I went to the mosque across from my house, Cerrahpasa Mosque, sat in the corner like a stranger, and as the call for prayer was being recited, I felt a deep sadness in my soul… It was as though a voice inside was saying to me, "*You're seeing the emptiness and meaninglessness of the world and everything in it, and none of this is fulfilling you, none of this is making you happy, try something different this time, try and see, you won't regret it….!*"

Suddenly, I made a decision. I decided to become a Muslim, to pray five times a day, to always have ablution and learn about the reality of Islam…

When I went home and shared this with my mother she cried with joy… She was so happy… Then I went back to the mosque for *Asr* and *Magrib* prayers… And I asked my next door neighbor, the late brother Jamal, if he knew of any books about Islam.

He gave me the 11 volume *Sahih Bukhari Hadith Collection*, and I read all 11 books at one go!

My world changed; it was as though I was transported to the time of the Rasul of Allah (saw) and I had become one of his family members, like I was living among them… By the way, I was immediately applying everything I was learning from the hadiths, though only in their 'literal' sense… I was fasting every day, attending every congregational prayer I could, opening the gates of the mosque at dawn for morning prayer, even reciting the call for prayer with my out of tune voice! All of this I was doing for the sake of ingratiating myself with my 'god'! I had even accepted that the earth is flat and the Nile was flowing towards the equator, all out of my pure unadulterated faith in those who spoke in the name of 'religion.'

I was spending my days in quiet retreat, constantly reading and researching. My other neighbor had brought me the eight volumes of the *Interpretation of the Quran* by Elmalili Hamdi Yazir. I was spending my days and nights reading the Quran and hadith, and giving English language lessons now and then to earn a few pennies.

My only purpose now was to serve my god and serve humanity in the way of the Rasul (saw).

Of course, I was also questioning everything I was learning; in fact, I had so many questions, that I was introduced first to the late Gonenli Mehmet Efendy, then to the late Sayyid Osman Efendy from Madina. In a short time, Sayyid Oman Efendy and I became like grandpa-grandson, he was so fond of me that he began to share esoteric knowledge with me. At this time, I had begun to read into Sufism. I read books by Abdulqadir al-Jilani, Imam Ghazali, Muhyiddin ibn al-Arabi and Sheikh Naqshibandi. My view and perspective was beginning to change… I was growing colder to the concept of a "god," but closer to understanding the reality denoted by the name Allah.

I was now looking for much deeper knowledge about the Unity of Existence. Shallow talks were not satisfying me. One day in the mosque a 106-year-old Naqshibandi Sheikh noticed me and asked me to go near him. He said, "Recite a hundred thousand *surat al-ikhlas* and come back to me." I immediately started reading the short chapter and in 20 days I completed a hundred thousand recitals. But I never saw him again, as he had passed on to the other realm during those 20 days…

My understanding of the 'external' (*zahir*) and 'internal' (*batin*) had now transformed, I was now evaluating everything in the light of oneness and unity. I penned my understanding and experience in my book *The Great Awakening* during this time.

The Great Awakening was like the seed of my understanding and vision today. It grew into the branches that became all the other books I wrote until now and its leaves were scattered throughout the world with the internet.

Indeed, throughout all these years I saw, time and time again, that just like my approach in the first years, the majority of people have a completely literal approach to religion. They put no effort into deciphering what the Quran is actually about.

They don't realize that words are merely like clothes, just as they point to something, they also cover it!

Most of the commands in the Quran are metaphoric and denote much more than their literal meaning.

"Don't look at what is illegitimate" for example means don't *desire* the illegitimate, where 'illegitimate' means *that which does not belong to you.*

"Condemn the action not the doer" for example is one of the most important and fundamental principles of Islam, yet so many are unaware of it.

The Sufi way derives its roots from Hadhrat Abu Bakr (ra) and Hadhrat Ali (ra), yet most people do not know the value of this sacred jewel.

Everyone has found a scholar or a sheikh for themselves, most of which have passed on, and they've conditioned themselves to their teachings, instead of realizing that they themselves are the direct addressees of Allah and the Quran.

Above all, we've come to a state where people are killing for the sake of their god! Announcing themselves to be the vicegerents of Allah, solely to satisfy their need for power, they are almost forcing people to pray and fast and cover their hair!

On the other hand, we see an Iranian type of "republic" approach or the old German "democratic" type regime where in the name of defending human rights people are controlled and manipulated into complying and obeying!

My God!

Will we ever see the days in which people will respect each other and not violate each other's rights???

Or are we not worthy of this?

Or is it simply that, "Every nation is governed in the way they deserve!"? …

23.5.99

54

SACRIFICE

Allah predetermines the sustenance of all creation before they are created. The sustenance of the servant will come to him in parts, from the point of his creation to infinity, according to what has been predetermined for him.

Whatever he needs in order to fulfill his servitude in a wholesome way, it is given to him at every instance. Depending on his creation and nature, he will do the necessary 'work' for this sustenance to come to him. Nobody can get an iota's worth extra or less than what has been determined. Saying "If only I had done this…" or "if I hadn't done that I would have earned more…" only shows one's lack of discernment of the system.

The blind is not one whose eyes don't see, but one who is unable to see the universal system and order!

Allah gives!

And sometimes, Allah wants a sacrifice!

And sometimes, redemption!

Sacrifice is for cleansing; redemption is for rescue.

But what about the leash you've put on yourself? If you can't take your leash off in this world, you will never be able to take it off in the next world.

That leash is called "I," and the only way to get it off is to pay its redemption. To *sacrifice* yourself!

Making a sacrifice is all about realizing the inexistence of your assumed identity-self and to annihilate it, to sacrifice it, to the Ever-Living One.

The wise like to give. They give unrequitedly.

The "I"-leashed love to take. And they never give without a return.

The morals of Allah are such that He sends the rain without a return, He gives the air without a return, He gave us eyes so we can observe His beauty without a return, He gave us hands so we can hold and enjoy beauty without a return…

Indeed, each will live what has been predetermined for him and each will live the results of his actions.

I can only deliver to you what has been predetermined for you, but the giver is always Allah. We will all succeed in what has been eased for us by creation. What we can't achieve is what has not been determined for us.

The rain falls upon many barren lands where nothing ever greens. But it doesn't stop raining…

Expectation is either from hope or from ignorance. Those who carry their grave on their backs have already abandoned the world… They are those who "flee to Allah"…

Anyway, my friends, I wish not to take up too much of your time…

Give unrequitedly without expecting a return… If need be, pay its redemption too, in fact, give your "I" away too!

To become moralized with the morals of Allah is to give away everything you own!

We came naked to this world; we're going to be naked when we go. Give away your world, your hereafter, even if it hurts, even if it burns you, give everything that makes you "you" away…

Purify yourself, just like gold is purified with fire, purify yourself from your self and reach the station of the Pure Self!

If this is what you've been created for, it will be eased for you, you will find yourself doing whatever is necessary in this way… But maybe, it's not going to be easy at all, maybe it's going to be hard to give, maybe it's going to burn you, maybe you're already burning… In any case, know that this is good for you, this is purifying you, burn yourself away and become completely free!

AHMED HULUSI

ABOUT THE AUTHOR

Ahmed Hulusi (Born January 21, 1945, Istanbul, Turkey) contemporary Islamic philosopher. From 1965 to this day he has written close to 30 books. His books are written based on Sufi wisdom and explain Islam through scientific principles. His established belief that the knowledge of Allah can only be properly shared without any expectation of return has led him to offer all of his works which include books, articles, and videos free of charge via his web-site. In 1970 he started examining the art of spirit evocation and linked these subjects parallel references in the Quran (smokeless flames and flames instilling pores). He found that these references were in fact pointing to luminous energy which led him to write *Spirit, Man, Jinn* while working as a journalist for the Aksam newspaper in Turkey. Published in 1985, his work called *The Human Enigma* (*Insan ve Sirlari*) was Hulusi's first foray into decoding the messages of the Quran filled with metaphors and examples through a scientific backdrop. In 1991 he published *The Power of Prayer* (*Dua and Zikir*) where he explains how the repetition of certain prayers and words can lead to the realization of the divine attributes inherent within our essence through increased brain capacity. In 2009 he completed his final work, '*Decoding the Quran, A Unique Sufi Interpretation*' which encompasses the understanding of leading Sufi scholars such as Abdulkarim al Jili, Abdul-Qadir Jilani, Muhyiddin Ibn al-Arabi, Imam Rabbani, Ahmed ar-Rifai, Imam Ghazali, and Razi, and which approached the messages of the Quran through the secret Key of the letter 'B'.

www.ingramcontent.com/pod-product-compliance
Lightning Source LLC
Chambersburg PA
CBHW031954040426
42448CB00006B/359

* 9 7 8 0 6 9 2 7 5 6 0 8 9 *